Study Guide for Book Clubs: Educated

KATHRYN COPE

CONTENTS

INTRODUCTION

There are few things more rewarding than getting together with a group of like-minded people and discussing a good book. Book club meetings, at their best, are vibrant, passionate affairs. Each member will bring along a different perspective and ideally there will be heated debate.

A surprising number of book club members, however, report that their meetings have been a disappointment. Even though their group loved the particular book they were discussing, they could think of astonishingly little to say about it. Failing to find interesting discussion angles for a book is the single most common reason for book group discussions to fall flat. Most book groups only meet once a month and a lacklustre meeting is frustrating for everyone.

Study Guides for Book Clubs were born out of a passion for reading groups. Packed with information, they take the hard work out of preparing for a meeting and ensure that your book group discussions never run dry. How you choose to use the guides is entirely up to you. The author biography and style sections provide useful background information which may be interesting to share with your group at the beginning of your meeting. The all-important list of discussion questions, which will probably form the core of your meeting, can be found towards the end of this guide. To support your responses to the discussion questions, you may find it helpful to refer to the Themes & Symbolism, Character, and Location sections.

A detailed plot synopsis is provided as an aide-memoire if you need to recap on the finer points of the plot. There is also a quick quiz - a fun way to test your knowledge and bring your discussion to a close. Finally, if this was a book that you particularly enjoyed, the guide concludes with a list of books similar in style or subject matter.

Study Guides for Book Clubs are intended to enhance your appreciation of the original novel. They are not a substitute for reading the real thing. As this guide contains spoilers, please don't be tempted to read it before you have read the original novel as plot surprises will be well and truly ruined.

Kathryn Cope, 2018

TARA WESTOVER

Tara Westover was born in 1986 in Idaho. Growing up in the shadow of her father - a Mormon extremist and survivalist - she first attended school when she was seventeen. She went on to scale the pinnacles of academic success, graduating from Brigham Young University in 2008, earning an MPhil from Trinity College, Cambridge in 2009, and receiving a doctorate from Harvard University in 2014. A direct consequence of this education, however, was an increasingly troubled relationship with her family. Westover's memoir, *Educated*, tells the story of this process.

On its release in February 2018, *Educated* became an international publishing sensation and shot into the New York Times Best Sellers list. The memoir has also received widespread critical acclaim.

While writing *Educated*, Tara Westover consulted the relatives she remained in touch with and used their real names in her memoir. Pseudonyms were used for family members she no longer saw (her parents and her siblings, Shawn, Audrey and Luke). Nevertheless, due to the success of her mother's essential oil business, a brief internet search reveals the identity of several of the key people mentioned in the book. *Educated* has received a hostile reception from Westover's estranged relatives who claim inaccuracies in her account.

The author now lives in the United Kingdom.

PLOT SYNOPSIS

Prologue

In 1993 Tara Westover is seven years old. Her family live in Buck's Peak, Idaho: a rural area that sits in the shadow of a mountain. One of seven children, Tara has been brought up in a Mormon household. She has never attended school as her father believes the education system is part of a government conspiracy to make children ungodly. Raised to believe in the Days of Abomination, she and her family await the end of the world and Christ's Second Coming.

PART ONE

1 – Choose the Good

Tara's perception of the world is influenced by an incident that occurs when she is just five years old. Her father, Gene, tells his children that Federal agents have killed an entire family at nearby Ruby Ridge. According to Gene, Randy Weaver, his wife, and their son were all shot dead. He claims that the Weavers were targeted as the government did not want them to home-educate their children. After hearing this story, Tara worries that the same thing will happen to her own family.

Two years later, Gene believes that he has received a revelation from God and bans dairy products from the family home. Tara sneaks over to see her paternal grandmother (grandma-down-the-hill) for milk.

Grandma-down-the-hill broaches a secret plan to Tara. She suggests that, as she and her husband spend the winters in Arizona, Tara could come with them and go to school. Agreeing to the plan, Tara gets up early the next day. When her grandparents arrive to pick her up, however, she decides that she cannot leave her family.

2 - The Midwife

Gene believes that conventional medicines are sinful. His wife, Faye, treats all ailments with herbs. Keen for Faye to extend her skills, he encourages her to assist the local midwife – a woman with no formal qualifications who attends home births. Faye is reluctant but Gene insists that it is her calling.

After months of assisting with births, Faye becomes the only unofficial midwife in the area when her mentor moves to Wyoming. Growing more self-assured in the role, she has a telephone installed at home without consulting her husband.

When she is nine years old, Tara attends a birth for the first time. The experience makes her realize that, if a mother or baby should die, her mother is at risk of going to prison for manslaughter. Shortly afterwards, Faye is forced to drive a mother to the hospital when her baby's heart rate drops dangerously low. Speeding, she attracts the attention of the police who escort her to the hospital. Questioned by hospital staff, Faye plays dumb, allaying any suspicions that she might be an unlicensed midwife. Afterwards, she revels in telling the story of how she fooled the police and medical establishment.

Due to Gene's objection to official registration with the government, his younger children (Tara, Audrey, Richard and Luke) do not possess birth certificates. When Luke is fifteen, he requires a birth certificate to enroll in Driver's Ed. Faye embarks on the process of applying for certificates on behalf of all four children. In Tara's case, this proves difficult as her family cannot agree on her birthdate. Eventually, she is issued with a Delayed Certificate of Birth.

3 – Cream Shoes

As a child, Tara finds it hard to equate her fearful father with photos of him as a carefree young man. While she has only ever known him as a zealous survivalist, her older brothers remember a time when he was less paranoid and allowed them to go to school.

4 - Apache Women

One winter, Gene becomes depressed, lying in bed every day without speaking. Believing that her husband needs sunshine, Faye decides that the family should travel to Arizona to stay with Gene's parents.

In Arizona, Gene begins to talk again, raving about conspiracies and "the Illuminati". After six days, he announces, during dinner, that it is time to make the twelve-hour drive home.

Driving through the night, seventeen-year-old Tyler falls asleep at the wheel, veers off the road and hits a tractor. Tara wakes up just as the car hits a utility pole. None of the Westovers wears a seatbelt and only Gene emerges from the accident relatively unscathed. Most seriously hurt is Tara's mother, whose facial contusions make her unrecognizable. The family are trapped beneath live power cables until the power company switch off the electricity. Recalling this incident as an adult, Tara thinks she remembers hearing her father ask if he should call an ambulance. She chooses to imagine that her mother made the request to go home.

For the next seven days, Faye lies in the dark basement of the family home. During this time, her facial swelling worsens. When she finally emerges, she has two large swellings on her forehead and dark rings around her eyes – prompting the children to refer to her as "Raccoon Eyes". After the accident, Faye often confuses her children's names and never quite returns to her normal self. Years later, Tara discovers that Raccoon Eyes is a medical term used to describe a symptom of brain damage.

5 – Honest Dirt

Tara's brother, Tyler, is noticeably different from the rest of his family. While the rest of the Westovers are happy to live in rowdy chaos, Tyler likes books, classical music and order. One day, Tyler plays Tara a recording of the Mormon Tabernacle Choir. Astounded at its beauty, she requests to hear it again and again. She and her brother bond over music and begin to listen to CDs together every evening.

Tyler announces that he is going to college and, despite his father's lectures on the brainwashing effects of education, refuses to change his mind. On departing for Brigham Young University (a Mormon college) he leaves ten-year-old Tara her favourite CD. For the next five years, Tara is rarely to see him.

Faye's mother is known to the Westover children as "grandma-over-in-town". Accustomed to hearing her father sneering at her maternal grandmother's respectable lifestyle, Tara shares his disrespectful view of her. One day, her perception momentarily changes when her grandma urges her to wash her hands after using the bathroom – something she has never been taught at home. For a moment, Tara takes the advice seriously. When her grandma confronts Gene about teaching his children personal hygiene, however, he unrepentantly declares that he has taught them "not to piss on their hands". Once again, Tara is converted to her father's viewpoint.

6 – Shield and Buckler

To avoid working for their father, Tara's older sister, Audrey, takes several jobs and is rarely at home. Struggling for a workforce, Gene enlists Tara and Richard to work as "crew" in his scrapyard.

Nine months after the car accident, Faye still suffers from migraines and problems with her memory. Nevertheless, she begins creating essential oil formulas for certain maladies using "muscle testing". This involves asking what an illness requires, picking up an oil, and waiting to see if her fingers click in response.

Between working in the scrapyard and helping her mother mix oils, Tara begins to study The Book of Mormon and the New Testament, making notes and writing essays. Whenever Gene catches his daughter studying, he finds more work for her to do. On one occasion, he asks her to water the fruit trees during a rainstorm. Meanwhile, Tara's brother, Richard, frequently escapes down the basement to read an encyclopedia.

One day, while working in the scrapyard, Gene instructs Tara to climb onto the loader – a huge forklift used to lift and drop bins of scrap metal. While up in the air, Tara becomes pinned to the bin by a metal spike which sticks in her leg. Unable to hear his daughter's cries, Gene empties the bin from the loader. As her leg tears free, Tara falls twenty-feet to the ground. On seeing that Tara is in shock and that her leg is badly gashed, Gene sends her back to the house to be treated by her mother. Through muscle testing, Faye establishes that Tara has damaged her kidney and treats the injury with herbs.

Determined to escape the scrapyard, Tara tells her father that she wants to go to school. Gene replies that her request is disloyal to both her family and God.

7 – The Lord Will Provide

On a hot summer's day, when Tara is ten years old, Faye leaves her daughter preparing oils while she goes to Utah. Meanwhile, Tara's seventeen-year-old brother, Luke, is on the mountain with his father helping to prepare cars for the crusher. Forgetting that he spilt gasoline on his jeans earlier in the day, Luke lights a cutting torch, engulfing his leg in flames. Unable to remove his jeans, he panics, running about and spreading fire through the dry undergrowth.

Tara first learns of the accident when Luke runs into the house screaming for their mother. Realizing that her brother is in shock and has suffered horrific burns to his leg, she tries to imagine what Faye would do. After giving Luke Rescue Remedy, Tara stands her brother in a large garbage can filled with water. To protect him from the blazing sun, she places a sombrero on his head and wraps a blanket around his shoulders.

When Faye returns from Utah, she reprimands Tara for using a garbage can. After muscle testing Luke's burn, however, she declares that it is not infected. Despite Faye's admission that she has never seen such a bad burn, there is no suggestion that Luke should go to the hospital. After responding well to Faye's homeopathic treatments, he returns to work in the scrapyard.

Years later, as she wrote her memoir, Tara noticed a gap in her understanding of the events surrounding Luke's accident. Contacting her brother, Richard, she asked him how Luke got back from the mountain and who put out the fire. Richard told her that their father put Luke in the truck and told him to drive home, while he stayed on the mountain to fight the fire in the undergrowth.

8 – Tiny Harlots

At the age of eleven, Tara decides the only way to escape the junkyard is to find other employment. Taking a job packing boxes of nuts, she also begins babysitting for several families. When she learns that one of her customers is a talented pianist, she asks for piano lessons in lieu of payment.

Guessing that Tara does not have any friends, her piano teacher suggests that she joins dance classes taught by her sister, Caroline. After Tara turns up to her first class wearing jeans and steel-toed boots, Caroline tells Faye that her daughter needs more appropriate dancewear. Faye buys Tara a leotard, tights and jazz shoes but advises her to keep them hidden in her room.

Familiar with her father's belief that women should reveal nothing above the ankles, Tara wears a knee-length T-shirt over her leotard but still feels exposed. As the Christmas dance recital looms, Faye informs Caroline that the costume is too revealing for Tara to wear. Caroline changes the costumes to oversized grey sweatshirts so that Tara can join in the performance.

On hearing about the dance recital, Gene insists on attending. Aware of her father's disapproving face in the audience, Tara is afraid to expose anything more of her legs and does not perform the moves she has learned. On the way home, Gene criticizes his wife for allowing their daughter to take part in a public display of sin. Agreeing with her husband, Faye claims she had no idea that the costumes would be so revealing. Tara is confused by this conversation, knowing that her mother had seen and approved the costumes beforehand.

With dance classes now off limits, Faye finds Tara a voice teacher. After singing a hymn in front of her church congregation, Tara is showered with praise. Revelling in the compliments his daughter receives, Gene glows with pride.

Hearing of an upcoming production of *Annie* in the nearest town, Tara's voice teacher suggests that her pupil auditions for the main role. Faye prepares her daughter for disappointment, convinced that her husband will not allow it. When Gene learns of the audition, however, he insists that Tara should go, promising to find the money for the travel costs.

9 - Perfect in His Generations

Having landed the starring role in *Annie*, Tara attends rehearsals at the Opera House in the small town of Worm Creek. This marks her first exposure to people from outside her church community. One of the people she meets is Charles – a friendly boy of a similar age. Although attracted to Charles's normalcy, Tara keeps her distance, imagining his reaction if she invited him home.

During every performance of *Annie*, Gene sits proudly in the front row. He goes on to allow Tara to perform in further plays, despite fearing that his daughter is mixing with corrupting influences.

As 1999 draws to a close, Gene becomes convinced that the Days of Abomination will begin with the year 2000. Spending all the family's income on firearms and supplies, he advises the rest of the community to do the same. On New Year's Eve, he waits expectantly for the electricity to fail and the world to fall into chaos. Believing her father's prophecy, Tara is puzzled when none of his predictions come to pass.

10 – Shield of Feathers

When the end of the world fails to materialize, Gene slips into another depression. Again, Faye prescribes a trip to Arizona. As before, Gene lays in the sun for several days before announcing that they will drive home through the night.

On the journey home, Richard drives through a snowstorm but eventually pulls over declaring it too treacherous to continue. Gene then takes the wheel and, as he drives recklessly fast, his terrified family await the inevitable crash. When the van veers off the road, Tara is knocked unconscious. An ambulance arrives but, frightened of being taken to the hospital, Tara omits to tell the medics that she lost consciousness.

A few days later, Tara is forced to take to her bed when she begins to suffer from a frozen neck and paralyzing headaches. After two weeks with no improvement, Faye calls an "energy specialist" who tells Tara to imagine herself inside a healing bubble. The advice proves useless, but Tara becomes accustomed to the headaches.

Soon afterwards, Tara's brother, Shawn, returns to Buck's Peak. Although Tara barely remembers him, she knows that Shawn has a reputation as a bully and a troublemaker. After telling Tara that she should see a chiropractor for her frozen neck, Shawn creeps up behind her, violently wrenching her head until it cracks. Tara collapses from the pain but realizes that she can turn her neck again.

11 – Instinct

Shawn volunteers to drive Tara to her rehearsals and they begin riding horses together. During this time, they develop a bond. One day, Tara gets into difficulties when her horse begins rearing and bucking. Although her instinct is to throw herself clear of the saddle, she holds on, feeling certain that her brother will save her. Sure enough, Shawn catches up with his sister on an unbroken horse and helps her to safely dismount.

12 – Fish Eyes

As the bond between them grows, Shawn teaches Tara martial arts. At Tara's rehearsals, a girl called Sadie begins to show interest in Shawn. Tara observes as her brother plays with Sadie's emotions, encouraging her one moment and humiliating her the next. His favourite game is to ask Sadie to fetch something, watch her obey him and then claim that he asked for something entirely different. Shawn begins to spy on Sadie, sometimes taking Tara with him. Soon, Sadie tells the boys at school not to approach her in case they provoke Shawn's displeasure.

One day, Shawn orders Tara to fetch him a glass of water, threatening to withhold her ride to rehearsals if she refuses. Tara obeys but pours the water over her brother's head when she sees his triumphant expression. In response, Shawn grabs his sister by the hair, shoves her head down the toilet and twists her wrist until she apologizes. Later the same day he tells Tara that he is sorry for his behaviour.

13 – Silence in the Churches

Tara first learns of the existence of the Twin Towers when they are destroyed in a terrorist attack. In the Westover household, 9/11 revives Gene's predictions of the end of the world. Meanwhile, Tara's nineteen-year-old sister, Audrey, marries Benjamin: a local farmer.

Fifteen-year-old Tara worries about becoming 'impure'. These

15

anxieties are largely prompted by Shawn. Disapproving of Tara's friendship with Charles and her experimentation with cosmetics, he calls her various names to imply that she is unwholesome and promiscuous.

Shawn's behaviour grows increasingly erratic. After dumping Sadie, he is irate when he learns that she has a date with Charles. Driving around the neighbourhood, he unsuccessfully searches for Charles with a pistol by his side. Shortly afterwards, Tara wakes up to find Shawn throttling her while accusing her of being "a slut". The attack continues as he drags her into the hallway by her hair, ignoring his mother's pleas to stop. Tara only escapes when Tyler unexpectedly returns home and confronts Shawn. Rather than feeling relieved, Tara is embarrassed that Tyler has witnessed Shawn's attack on her.

Shawn presents Tara with a pearl necklace, declaring that he does not want her to become like other women. Meanwhile, Tyler advises Tara to leave home as soon as possible. He suggests she should focus on passing the ACT which will allow her to apply for Brigham Young University.

14 - My Feet No Longer Touch Earth

Tara has always assumed that she will marry and become a midwife, like her mother. For this reason, she does not initially take Tyler's advice seriously. She changes her mind when her brother suggests that she could study music and become director of the church choir. Buying an ACT guide, she begins to study in earnest.

Shawn criticizes his father's dangerous working methods on a regular basis. One day, he proves his own point when he falls off an elevated wooden pallet. Landing, headfirst, on a concrete wall, Shawn suffers brain damage. Gene, however, leaves his son to rest and continues working - apparently unaware of the severity of Shawn's injuries. It becomes clear that something is seriously wrong when Shawn launches himself at his father, screaming. Together, Gene, Luke and Benjamin subdue Shawn but, in the process, Shawn hits his head a second time. One of the crew dials 9-11 and Shawn is airlifted to hospital.

Shawn survives his critical injuries, but it is unclear how badly the accident has affected his brain function. Observing that he has displayed violent tendencies in the hospital, doctors suggest that the accident might have altered Shawn's personality. Once home, Shawn's rages intensify, and Tara regularly cleans the toilet, knowing that her head may soon be in it.

Looking back, Tara is unconvinced that the accident significantly changed Shawn's behaviour. Reading her journals from the time, she realizes that she wanted to convince herself that Shawn's sadism was something new.

15 – No More a Child

Tara remains divided between wanting to go to college and pleasing her father. After Gene declares that she is incurring God's "wrath", Tara tells her mother that she has changed her mind about going to BYU. Faye surprises Tara with her response, privately urging her daughter not to let anything stand in the way of her plans. Tara goes ahead and sits the ACT test but feels sure that she has failed.

One day, in the scrapyard, Luke rips his shirt to cool himself down in the hot sun. Also overheated, Tara rolls up the sleeves of her T-shirt, baring a small area of her shoulders. Gene immediately yanks her sleeves back down again, criticizing her lack of modesty. When Tara rolls her sleeves back up he looks perplexed at this challenge to his authority.

As soon as Tara starts saving for college tuition, her father begins charging her for various living expenses. When she discovers that she has achieved a good score on the ACT (although not high enough for entry to BYU), Gene responds by telling her to move out. Calculating her daughter to be around twenty, Faye agrees with her husband until Tara reminds her that she is only sixteen.

Gene brings home a metal-cutting machine called 'the Shear'. Refusing to use the lethal-looking contraption, Shawn storms off. This leaves Luke next-in-line to try it. Within five minutes of using the Shear, Luke gashes his arm and runs to the house to be tended to by Faye. Unperturbed, Gene asks Benjamin to take Luke's place, but he refuses. With only Tara remaining, Gene tells his daughter to step up. Shawn returns to the yard just as Tara is thrown to the floor by the force of the Shear. Furious, Shawn tells his father that his little sister should not be using the machine. Gene, however, replies that if Tara does not use the Shear she cannot continue to live in his house. Eventually, Shawn backs down but takes the most dangerous role himself, asking Tara to pass him the iron, while he feeds the Shear. They continue to work the machine together for the next month. During this time, Shawn receives several more head injuries.

16 – Disloyal Man, Disobedient Heaven

One evening, after watching a movie at grandma-down-the-hill's house, Shawn drives off on his motorcycle while Tara follows in the car. On the way back, she stops when she sees a crowd gathered around the site of an accident. The injured person is Shawn who has suffered another head injury after hitting a cow in the road. The wound is so deep that it reveals his brain.

Tara calls her father for advice. Even after she has described the extent of Shawn's injuries, however, Gene tells her to bring her brother home. Ignoring her father's instructions, Tara drives Shawn to the hospital where a CAT scan reveals his injury is not as serious as it looks. Afterwards, Gene does not comment on Tara's disobedience but refuses to look at her. Recognizing this as a turning point in her relationship with her father, Tara commits herself to leaving Buck's Peak.

Tara's application to BYU is accepted after she achieves an excellent score in her second ACT test. Faye drives her daughter to Utah to help her find accommodation and, on their return, they find Gene in a temper. After accusing Tara of disconnecting the VCR cables, he becomes even angrier when Faye admits that she was responsible. Panicking, Tara begins trying to reconnect the cables as her father continues to shout. Then, in a moment of clarity, she abandons the task and walks out of the room. Faye takes her daughter's place on the floor, struggling to reconnect the VCR.

PART TWO

17 – To Keep It Holy

On New Year's Day, seventeen-year-old Tara moves into her apartment near Brigham Young University. Her reaction on meeting her fellow housemates is one of shock. Although Shannon and Mary are also Mormons, their interpretation of the faith is much more liberal. Wearing clothes that Tara considers immodest, her housemates also violate the Sabbath. Horrified, Tara isolates herself from the other girls.

In classes, Tara feels totally out of her depth as the gaps in her knowledge become apparent. In an art history lesson, she puts up her hand to ask the meaning of "Holocaust" and is surprised when her query is met with a disapproving silence. At the first opportunity, Tara searches "Holocaust" on the Internet. She is shocked by the facts and the extent of her own ignorance.

18 – Blood and Feathers

Tara proves unpopular with her BYU housemates. Accustomed to living in a dirty home, she fails to do her share of the chores. Her personal hygiene also becomes an issue, as she only uses soap twice a week when she showers.

With her finances dwindling, Tara researches the requirements for a scholarship and discovers that she would need an almost perfect GPA to receive one. This seems an unattainable goal as she has already failed her first Western Civilization exam. Calling home, she admits to her father that she is finding college challenging. Gene surprises his daughter with reassurances and a pledge that he will try to help if she fails to get a scholarship.

Tara's only friend at college is Vanessa and they study for the next Western Civilization exam together. When it emerges that Tara has only been studying the pictures, Vanessa reveals that students are expected to read the textbook as well. From this point on, Vanessa distances herself from Tara. Armed with this new knowledge, however, Tara begins to achieve good grades.

19 – In the Beginning

At the end of the semester, Tara goes home to Buck's Peak for the summer. Wary of sliding back into old routines, she takes a job at the grocery store to avoid working for her father. Her parents insist, however, that she cannot stay with them if she does not help in the junkyard. Quitting the grocery store job, she begins to feel as if she never left home.

After bumping into Charles, Tara agrees to see a movie with

him. They start seeing each other regularly and Tara hopes for a romance. When Charles touches her, however, she thinks of Shawn accusing her of impurity and pulls away.

20 – Recitals of the Fathers

Feeling that university has given Tara ideas above her station, Shawn and Gene do their best to bring her down a peg or two. While her father dishes out unreasonable orders, Shawn calls her "Nigger." Although Tara has heard members of her family use the "N" word before, she had never previously dwelled on its meaning. Now aware of the history of slavery and the civil rights movement, Tara finds she can no longer laugh off her brother's casual racism.

21 – Skullcap

Before returning to BYU, Tara suffers from an excruciating earache. Charles offers her painkillers, but she is reluctant to take them, remembering her mother's warnings about the devastating effects of conventional medicine. Eventually accepting the painkillers, she is amazed at how effective they are.

Back at university, Tara moves into a new apartment with different roommates. One of the housemates - Robin – seems to understand Tara's ignorance of societal norms and gently coaches her in cleaning and basic hygiene.

Although in receipt of a scholarship for half her tuition fees, Tara struggles to make ends meet and works as a janitor to pay the rent. Terrified of losing her scholarship after failing a midterm algebra exam, she stops sleeping in order to study. She develops stomach ulcers and, one day, one of her housemates finds her prostrate with pain between the campus and their apartment. Nevertheless, Tara refuses to go to the hospital.

On Charles's advice, Tara goes to see her algebra professor and tells him that if she fails his class, she will lose her scholarship. The professor promises that, if she achieves a perfect score on the final exam paper, he will forget her midterm failure.

22 – What We Whispered and What We Screamed

Tara returns to Buck's Peak for Thanksgiving, inviting Charles to have dinner with her family. Halfway through the meal, Shawn makes Tara drop a plate of food. As soon as Tara protests, Shawn pins his sister to the floor before dragging her to the bathroom by the hair and shoving her head in the toilet. Throughout the assault, Tara focuses on convincing Charles that he is witnessing normal sibling high jinks, laughing dementedly as Shawn hurts her. Even after she falls into the bath, breaking her big toe, Tara assures Charles that she is fine. Afterwards, Tara feels angry with Charles for witnessing her humiliation. When they meet, she pushes him away and Charles eventually declares that, although he loves her, he cannot save her – only she can do that.

Back at university, stomach ulcers cause Tara to shout out in her sleep and her big toe turns black. When Robin offers to take her to a doctor, however, Tara refuses. She also rejects her friend's advice to consult the bishop of their church or go for counselling. After studying intensely, she achieves a perfect score in her algebra paper.

Tara returns to Buck's Peak for Christmas to find her father encouraging Richard to take the ACT test. Gene declares that his son is "a genius" but Richard confides to Tara that he achieved a poor result on the practice ACT test.

One day, Tara and Shawn drive to the grocery store and notice Charles's jeep parked outside. Suddenly conscious of her dishevelled appearance, Tara tells her brother that she will wait in the car. In response, Shawn drags Tara onto the ground, pins her arms above her head, exposing her underwear, and bends her arm back until she screams. When people turn to stare, Tara laughs hysterically and continues to do so as Shawn walks her around the store. They do not bump into Charles.

Later, Shawn apologizes to Tara, claiming that he did not know he had hurt her. Replaying the incident in her mind, Tara realizes that Shawn took pleasure in humiliating her. For the first time, she writes a completely honest account of Shawn's behaviour in her journal.

When Tara returns to BYU, she receives a further apology from Shawn by email. In her journal, she finds the entry for that day and, on the opposite page, writes a note to say that the incident was a misunderstanding. She does not, however, amend her original description of the assault and its aftermath.

23 – I'm from Idaho

Continuing to identify with Shawn's definition of her as a "whore", Tara avoids relationships with men. After refusing two different suitors from her church, she gains a reputation for being anti-marriage. As a result, she is summoned by the bishop who she finds surprisingly easy to confide in. At the end of the semester, the bishop urges her not to go back to Buck's Peak and adds that, if money is the issue, the church will pay her rent. Tara refuses the offer out of pride but promises that she will not work for her father.

In Buck's Peak, Tara returns to working at the grocery store. She also learns that Shawn has a new girlfriend called Emily. Tara is dismayed to see that her brother is just as controlling and manipulative with Emily as he was with Sadie.

After going back to university, Tara suffers an excruciating toothache and is forced to visit a dentist. Unable to afford the $1400 required for root canal surgery, she calls her parents. Faye agrees to loan Tara the money, but Gene attaches a clause – she will have to work for him the following summer. Tara turns down the offer, telling her parents she will never work in the junkyard again.

When the bishop hears about Tara's dental emergency, he suggests she should apply for a grant. Remembering her father's lectures on the evils of government handouts, Tara rejects the suggestion. She also turns down the bishop's offer to pay for her dentistry work.

Soldiering on with her painful tooth, Tara continues to struggle for money. Just as she decides to quit university for a full-time job, Shawn unexpectedly gives her $100 as a Christmas gift. She continues her studies while working in a diner and taking a second job as a cleaner.

When the bishop once again urges Tara to apply for a grant, she relents. Knowing that her father will not willingly hand over the tax returns required for her application, she decides to steal them. Arriving at Buck's Peak in the early hours of the morning, Tara is confronted by Shawn who is sitting in the dark and holding a pistol. The next day Tara asks her mother for the tax returns and Faye hands them over.

Tara's application for a grant proves successful. On receipt of a cheque for $4,000, she queries the amount, pointing out that she only needs $1400. Told that she has two options – to cash it or not – Tara opts for the former. She finally has her dental work done and, for the first time, feels confident that she will not have to return to working for her father.

24 – A Knight, Errant

When Tara first hears the term "bipolar disorder" in a psychology lecture, she realizes that the symptoms (paranoia, depression, etc.), describe her father. During the same lecture, another student asks about the role mental illness might have played in certain conflicts, including the Ruby Ridge siege.

After the lecture, Tara researches the Ruby Ridge siege. She learns that the incident began as a covert surveillance operation by Federal agents on Randy Weaver's property. The operation began to go wrong when the Weavers' dog detected the presence of the agents. Armed with a gun, fourteen-year-old Sammy Weaver went to investigate. In the ensuing confrontation, gunfire was exchanged, and Sammy and his dog were killed. Shortly afterwards, Federal agents shot Randy Weaver in the arm and, when his wife went to help him (holding her baby daughter), government agents shot her in the head. The standoff lasted a further nine days until Randy Weaver was finally arrested. In the aftermath of the siege, the government was widely criticized for the handling of Ruby Ridge. Randy Weaver and his three surviving daughters sued and settled out of court, receiving $3 million between them.

In researching the siege, Tara is struck by the anomalies between her father's story and the reported facts. She is surprised to learn that Randy and his daughters survived, as she remembers Gene claiming that the entire Weaver family had been killed. She also discovers that the FBI's reason for targeting the Weavers was nothing to do with homeschooling. According to newspaper reports, it was Randy Weaver's association with a white supremacist group and the fact that he had sold sawed-off shotguns to an undercover agent that had led to the surveillance operation. Reeling from this new information, Tara assumes that her father must have deliberately lied to his family. She then recalls Gene's genuine fear after the siege and realizes that, after hearing about Ruby Ridge, he must have interpreted events according to his own paranoid beliefs.

Going home for the weekend, Tara furiously confronts her father about the way he distorted the events of Ruby Ridge and frightened his family. Gene responds with helpless astonishment. Returning to university, Tara ignores her father's calls and decides that she wants no further contact with him. When the summer holidays arrive, she does not return to Buck's Peak.

After trying out a new church, Tara begins dating Nick – a member of the congregation. When she falls ill, Nick presses Tara to consult a doctor and she attends a clinic for the first time. On learning that Tara has been prescribed penicillin, Faye sends tinctures to flush the antibiotics from her daughter's system – but nothing for Tara's sore throat.

Tara receives a call from Audrey to say that their father has had a serious accident. Audrey advises her sister to come home and say goodbye while she still can.

25 – The Work of Sulphur

Tara learns that, after forgetting to drain a car's fuel tank in the scrapyard, Gene had been at the centre of an explosion. As a result, he had suffered horrific burns to his face and hands but refused conventional medical treatment. As Gene's mouth and throat were too badly scorched to swallow liquids, Faye had hydrated her husband with an enema. She also cut away his dead skin, covering him with salve. Gene's heart stopped twice during the early days of his treatment but, when Tara arrives in Buck's Peak, he is still alive. She helps to nurse and feed her father.

26 - Waiting for Moving Water

After remaining bedridden for two months, it becomes clear that Gene will survive. For the first time, he begins to listen to Tara rather than lecturing her and takes an interest in her life at BYU. Tara feels it marks a new beginning for them.

Shawn announces his engagement to Emily and, shortly afterwards, Tara accompanies the couple on a camping trip. Alone with Emily, Tara tries to broach the subject of her brother's abusive behaviour. Emily admits that she is frightened of Shawn and that she believes that Satan is tempting him. When Tara suggests that she should not marry a man she is scared of, however, Emily clams up.

On returning to BYU, Tara cannot be honest with Nick about her family circumstances and ends their relationship. Leading up to Shawn's wedding, she feels that she should do something to prevent the marriage but takes no action.

27 - If I Were a Woman

Tara drops music to study geography, history and politics but feels conflicted about her decision. Unsure of whether she should be drawn to these 'unfeminine' subjects, she seeks advice from her professor, Dr. Kerry. Dr. Kerry suggests that Tara should apply for a study abroad program at Cambridge University in England.

Tara returns home for Christmas. Six months after her father's accident, his lungs remain damaged, his face is badly scarred, and his right hand is almost unusable. Nevertheless, it is generally agreed that his recovery is miraculous, and the recipe Faye used on his burns has become known as "Miracle Salve." Convinced that God planned both the accident and his recovery, Gene is consumed by religious fervour. Meanwhile, thanks to the apparent confirmation of her extraordinary healing powers, Faye has taken on a new air of confidence. In the background, Emily carries out heavy work for Faye's booming essential oil business, despite being pregnant and feeling unwell.

Offered a place on the program at the University of Cambridge, Tara has difficulties applying for a passport with her Delayed Certificate of Birth. Her application is finally approved after her Aunt Debbie swears an affidavit confirming Tara's identity.

After only twenty-six weeks of pregnancy, Emily goes into labour and gives birth to a baby boy named Peter. Weighing only one pound, four ounces when he is born, Peter undergoes months of surgery and remains frail. Tara's parents view the circumstances of his birth as a miracle orchestrated by God.

28 – Pygmalion

Arriving in Cambridge, Tara feels out of place amidst the ancient university's grandeur. Her insecurity momentarily evaporates, however, on a tour of a chapel roof. As the other students look unsteady and anxious, she stands tall. When Dr. Kerry observes this change in her, Tara explains that her confidence comes from roofing many hay sheds. She interprets the professor's comment as a further sign that she does not belong at Cambridge.

Tara decides to study historiography (the writing of history) and is assigned Professor Steinberg as her supervisor. When she submits her first essay, Professor Steinberg declares it to be one of the best he has ever read. He also tells Tara that he will ensure she is accepted to whichever graduate school she applies to. Dr. Kerry also continues to assure Tara that she deserves to be at Cambridge. Despite the praise of these eminent academics, she continues to lack faith in herself, unable to reconcile the idea of herself as a scholar with Shawn's definition of her as a "whore".

29 – Graduation

On returning to BYU, Tara applies for a scholarship at Cambridge. Meanwhile, her parents visit her at the university for the first time. During a meal at a restaurant, Gene loudly declares that World War II and the Holocaust were engineered by Jewish bankers. He then begins preaching about the end of the world. Out of the context of Buck's Peak, Tara finds her father's behaviour surreal and cannot understand why she used to believe everything he said.

Tara is offered a scholarship at the University of Cambridge. Interviewed by local newspapers about the achievement, she evades questions about where she went to school.

When Tara next visits Buck's Peak, her father is annoyed that she did not mention being homeschooled in her interviews. He expresses his disapproval of her plan to return to Cambridge. He also tells Tara that he is looking forward to meeting her professors at graduation so that he can give them a piece of his mind. When Tara protests, Gene retorts that he will not go where he is not welcome.

Although Tara receives the "most outstanding undergraduate" award from the history department, her parents do not turn up to graduation dinner at BYU. Calling her mother, Tara learns that they will not attend graduation unless she apologizes. Tara does so, conceding that her father can say whatever he wants. By the time Gene and Faye arrive, most of the graduation ceremony is over. Later, Tara's parents take her to the airport. Her father looks lost as she prepares to board a plane to England.

PART THREE

30 – Hand of the Almighty

As a graduate student at Cambridge, Tara realizes that, although she has physically left Buck's Peak, she is still mentally constrained by her father's beliefs. Making an active effort to immerse herself in her new life, Tara makes friends and finally has her vaccinations. Reading feminist literature, she begins to understand how women are often forced into roles that may be completely alien to their nature.

Returning to Buck's Peak for Christmas, Tara is surprised to find that a huge extension has been added to the house – funded by the success of her mother's essential oil business. One bitterly cold evening, Emily bursts into the house wearing no coat or shoes. Crying, she reveals that she has walked there in the snow as Shawn threw her out of their trailer when she returned home with the wrong crackers for their son. Embarrassed that Richard's wife, Kami, is witnessing the scene, Tara suggests that they should all go to their rooms and let Gene deal with the situation.

31 – Tragedy Then Farce

Before returning to England, Tara visits her sister, Audrey. When Audrey's children squabble over a toy, Tara takes it away from them saying "If you act like a child, ... I'll treat you like one." Shocked at hearing her sister use this phrase, Audrey points out that it was something that Shawn often said.

Back at university, Tara makes a determined effort to fit in, trying wine and wearing more fashionable clothes. After a trip to Rome with fellow students, she receives an email from Audrey. In her message, Audrey admits that Shawn was abusive towards her and expresses guilt that she did not stop the same thing from happening to Tara. She also reveals that, just before her marriage, she told their mother about Shawn's behaviour, but Faye claimed that her memories were false. Audrey says that she plans to confront Shawn and her parents and Tara responds, agreeing to support her.

27

Soon afterwards, Tara receives an email from her mother apologizing for failing to protect her from Shawn. Promising to speak to Gene about Shawn's bullying of his sisters and wife, Faye assures her daughter that the situation will be dealt with. Suddenly feeling free of a great burden, Tara begins to be more open with friends about her family background.

32 – A Brawling Woman in a Wide House

Tara begins dating her friend Drew and receives the news that she has earned a place at Cambridge to study for a doctorate. In the autumn, she returns to Buck's Peak to visit Grandma-down-the-hill who is dying of cancer.

After his mother's death, Gene sinks into depression, staying in bed while his wife juggles the business (whose employees now overrun the house) and funeral arrangements. One day Tara overhears her mother standing up to her father over the division of household chores. The following morning, Tara walks in on her father making his own breakfast. On seeing his daughter, he immediately delegates the task to her.

33 – Sorcery of Physics

Just before Tara returns to England, Audrey pleads with her not to go as she is afraid of confronting Shawn alone. Tara points out that her sister can depend upon their mother's support. Audrey claims, however, that, in the end, their parents did not believe the truth about Shawn.

At Christmas, Tara returns to Buck's Peak and goes for a drive with Shawn. Pulling into a deserted parking lot, Shawn rants about Audrey's betrayal of him. Calling Audrey a liar, he claims that he would shoot her if it were not a waste of a bullet. Frozen with fear, Tara says nothing, expecting her brother to assault her. Instead, Shawn suggests watching a movie and drives them home.

34 – The Substance of Things

Tara tells her parents that Shawn has threatened to shoot Audrey. In response, Gene accuses Tara of trying to create trouble for her brother and demands proof that Shawn is violent and manipulative.

Tara replies that no proof is needed as both of her parents have witnessed it. Throughout the conversation, Faye remains silent, failing to back her daughter up. Crying, Tara escapes to the bathroom. In her absence, Gene calls Shawn to tell him what his sister has accused him of.

Shortly afterwards, Shawn arrives and presents Tara with a bloodied knife. He tells her to use it on herself to spare the agony of what he plans to do to her. He is placated, however, when Tara claims that their father must have misunderstood what she said.

Tara leaves her parents' house first thing the next morning. On the way, she drives past Shawn and Emily's trailer and notices that the snow by their door is stained with blood. Later, she learns that the blood belonged to Diego: Shawn and Emily's German Shepherd. After Gene called Shawn with the news of Tara's betrayal, her brother had killed the family pet with a knife.

Looking back on the visit, Tara realizes that her mother lied to her. Despite claiming that she had raised the issue of Shawn's behaviour with Gene, she had never actually done so.

35 – West of the Sun

Back in Cambridge, Tara receives repeated calls from Shawn threatening to kill her or pay to have her murdered. When she tells her parents about the threats, Gene asks for evidence while Faye reassures her that Shawn cannot afford to hire a hitman. Both deny that Shawn threatened her with a bloodied knife, claiming that her memory of events is inaccurate. In a long accusatory email, Shawn tells Tara that he wants no further contact with her.

That summer, Tara is awarded a grant to study in Paris. While there, she receives an email from Audrey who has recently been visited by their father. During his visit, Gene claimed that Shawn had been cleansed of sin and had urged Audrey to forgive her brother. Audrey tells Tara that she has forgiven Shawn and now realizes that her sister is a bad influence. She concludes by asking Tara not to contact her again.

Knowing that her father will influence the rest of her siblings, Tara believes that she has lost her entire family. Beginning to blame her education for this loss, she feels no pleasure in learning that she has won a visiting fellowship to Harvard.

Thanks to her parents' alternative version of events, Tara begins to doubt her own memories and judgment. Writing to Shawn's former girlfriend, Erin, she asks for her recollections of her brother's behaviour. Erin confirms that Shawn was prone to rages and would often call her a "whore". She also recalls an incident when Shawn slammed her head against a wall and choked her until her grandpa intervened. Temporarily reassured that Erin's memories concur with her own, Tara then begins to wonder if Shawn's ex-girlfriend might also be mad. Four years later, this doubt is put to rest when she meets Erin's cousin by chance. Confirming that he witnessed Shawn viciously assaulting his cousin, he claims that, without the intervention of Erin's grandfather, the attack would have been fatal.

36 – Four Long Arms, Whirling

Tara begins her PhD at Harvard, deciding to study the conflict between an individual's obligation to family and their responsibilities to society. Reconnecting with Charles via an Internet chat room, she tells him about the rift with her family. Charles suggests that she should accept the situation, but Tara remains adamant that a reconciliation is possible.

Tara's parents visit her at Harvard, determined to convert her back to the Lord. After staying with her for a week, her father offers his daughter "a priesthood blessing" to cleanse her of the devil. Up until this point, Tara had decided she would go along with her parents' plan. When this moment finally arrives, she is surprised to find herself refusing. Although she wants to reconcile with her family Tara realizes that, in order to do so, she must sacrifice her independence of thought. Gene and Faye leave immediately, refusing to stay one more night in their daughter's presence.

37 - Gambling for Redemption

Tara suffers a mental breakdown. Giving up socializing and studying, she stays in her room watching TV. At night, she often wakes screaming and finds herself outside in her pyjamas.

Buying a ticket to Idaho for Christmas, Tara comes to the decision that she will accept her father's blessing after all. When Drew discovers her plans, he begs her not to go, pointing out that

Shawn might kill her. Tara ignores this advice. She also ignores the clear message of an ominous dream in which she is lying on a gurney while her father tells the police that she has stabbed herself.

Tara is greeted enthusiastically by Faye when she arrives in Buck's Peak. When Tara uses her mother's computer, however, she sees an email sent by Faye to Shawn's ex-girlfriend, Erin. The email claims that Shawn has been reborn while Tara is a danger to the family. It also reveals the 'miraculous' news that Emily has survived after a near-death experience giving birth to a daughter at home. Tara decides to leave but tells her mother she is just going for a drive. Seeming to intuit her intentions, her parents hug her, and Gene tells his daughter that he loves her.

Shortly after leaving Buck's Peak, Tara receives a call from Tyler. He tells his sister that their mother has been in touch with an unconvincing story about Shawn, a knife and a dead dog. As a previous victim of Shawn's bullying, Tyler pledges his support to Tara.

After visiting Drew in the Middle East, Tara returns to university but continues to suffer from nightmares, sleepwalking and panic attacks. In an angry letter to her father, she tells him that she needs to sever contact with him. Her mother responds, trying to change Tara's mind.

38 – Family

Still unable to study, Tara is in danger of failing her PhD. Meanwhile, Tyler tries to negotiate with his parents over the situation with Tara and Shawn. Agreeing that something needs to be done about Shawn, Faye claims that she has convinced Gene to take action. When Tyler speaks to his father, however, Gene threatens to disown him if he ever mentions Shawn's behaviour again. Shortly afterwards, Tyler receives a call from Shawn warning him that he could have him ejected from the family. Tara confidently expects Tyler to succumb to her parents' will. Instead, she receives a letter from Tyler which has also been sent to Faye and Gene. In the letter, Tyler and his wife, Stefanie, support Tara and condemn Faye and Gene for their unchristian behaviour.

Tara starts using the university's counselling service and, almost a year later, finds that she can think clearly enough to study. After submitting her PhD on her twenty-seventh birthday, she receives official confirmation that she has the right to call herself Dr. Westover. She moves into a flat in London with Drew.

39 - Watching the Buffalo

Tara returns to Buck's Peak to see Grandma-over-in-town when her Alzheimer's becomes so bad that she is transferred to a hospice. She discovers that, in her absence, her parents have become one of the biggest employers in the county.

Tara goes to see her grandfather but, when he talks about her parents as "great healers", she realizes there is no hope of a continued relationship between them. She also sends a note to her mother, asking if the two of them can meet. Faye refuses to see her daughter alone.

When her grandmother dies, Tara goes to stay with her Aunt Angie, who is also estranged from Tara's parents. Before the funeral, Tara meets aunts and uncles she has not seen since childhood. From them, she discovers that, over the years, Faye cut herself off from her siblings by always taking Gene's part. Reclaiming those relatives her mother has rejected, Tara begins to feel part of a family again. She also realizes, from the stories of her uncles and aunts, that Grandma-over-in-town was neither petty nor "frivolous".

Seeing her siblings at her grandmother's funeral, Tara feels a clear divide has developed between those who have left Buck's Peak and earned doctorates (herself, Richard and Tyler) and those who did not gain high school diplomas and now work for their parents. Audrey tells Tara that she is committing a great sin by refusing contact with their father. Before she leaves for London, Tara repeats her request to see Faye alone. Again, her mother refuses.

40 – Educated

By the end of her memoir, Tara has not seen her parents since her grandmother's funeral. She has, however, maintained a close relationship with Tyler, Richard and Tony. Although she does not know if the rift with her parents is permanent, she reflects that it has brought her "peace".

STYLE

The memoir is a literary genre that never goes out of fashion. Its continued popularity is a testament to our innate curiosity about the lives of others and the factors that make people who they are. Celebrity autobiographies continue to be a guaranteed source of income for publishers. Recent years, however, have also seen a boom in memoirs written by unknown authors.

In the run-up to Donald Trump's election, J.D. Vance's *Hillbilly Elegy* (2016) soared to the top of the book charts and became a subject of hot debate. Written by a Yale law graduate, the memoir described the author's impoverished childhood in a rural community of Ohio. The victim of domestic violence inflicted by his drug-addicted mother, Vance eventually escaped a bleak-looking future by joining the Marines and going to university. The book caused controversy as, in the process of telling his story, the author suggests that the ingrained poverty that prevails in the USA's 'Rust Belt' can partly be blamed on the "learned helplessness" of hillbilly culture.

Hot on the heels of *Hillbilly Elegy's* success came the 2017 film adaptation of Jeanette Walls' *The Glass Castle*. Walls' memoir is another fascinating account of rising above a dysfunctional and poverty-stricken American childhood – in her case to become a journalist.

Educated has much in common with *Hillbilly Elegy* and *The Glass Castle* as it is shocking and inspirational in equal measure. Although written at the tender age of twenty-nine, Westover's memoir charts an extraordinary life involving abuse, religious fundamentalism and mental illness. A celebration of the resilience of the human spirit, it is also an account of surviving one's dysfunctional upbringing (although not without scars).

While *Educated* describes harrowing events, it is far from a misery memoir. Although Westover recounts the details of horrific accidents, her brother's abusive behaviour, and her parents' failures to protect her, she does so without self-pity. Her narrative voice is matter-of-fact – reflecting the fact that, at the time, these incidents were her normality.

Avoiding melodrama, Westover also employs wit and humour as she recognizes the ridiculous nature of the scenarios she describes. While readers may be horrified at the idea of ten-year-old Tara treating Luke's burns alone, Westover sees surreal humour in the image of her brother standing in a bin with a sombrero on his head and a blanket around his shoulders. She is also able to laugh at the priggishness of her former self, describing with amusement the way she fled in horror after seeing the word "Juicy" emblazoned across the rear of her BYU roommate.

If *Educated* had been written in a workaday style, the facts of Westover's life would be enough to keep readers gripped. It is the artistry behind the author's prose, however, that elevates this memoir above many books in this genre. Although the story is based on fact, Westover writes like a novelist. One of the ways that this is evident is in the skilful shaping of the narrative. Rather than giving a blow-by-blow account of her formative years, the author selects only those episodes which most vividly illustrate her life – from her father's account of the Ruby Ridge Siege to the moment when she raises her hand in class to ask what "Holocaust" means. Each episode she chooses either conveys the nature of her family dynamics or its impact upon her. It is through these vignettes of family life that the author also carefully illustrates character. Despite the difficulties of objectively depicting family members, Westover ensures that her personal involvement in the story does not lead to the creation of two-dimensional heroes and villains. While she describes incidents that do not reflect well on her father, her mother, and Shawn, there are also moments that surprize us: her mother buying her a dance outfit, Shawn's courageous rescue of her on horseback, and her father's pride whenever she sings in public. Westover does not pass judgement on her family but shows them in all their contradictory complexity, letting readers draw their own conclusions. She is also careful not to whitewash her own failings, describing with great honesty how, time and again, she was complicit in Shawn's abusive behaviour.

One of the reasons for the enduring popularity of memoirs is that they present themselves as the truth. The idea that the author is sharing real events immediately creates a sense of intimacy with the reader. In reality, however, even the most frankly written memoir can only ever be a representation of one person's truth. By nature, memories are slippery and unreliable. This is because they are filtered through subjectivity (what a person chooses to remember) and the passage of time (the difficulty of accurately remembering dialogue etc.)

In *Educated*, Westover not only acknowledges the unreliability of memory but actively draws attention to it. Realizing that there were gaps in her memories of certain events, she consulted her brothers, Tyler and Richard during the writing process. Nevertheless, in her footnotes, she acknowledges that in the case of two particular accidents (Luke's burns and Shawn's fall) each of the family had a slightly different recollection of events. Also, although much of *Educated* is based on her childhood journals, Westover admits that these diaries did not always represent the truth. Reading her childhood writings with the benefit of hindsight, she acknowledges that they often attempt to conceal the unpalatable facts about Shawn's behaviour. Writing *Educated*, therefore, involves reinterpreting her journals by identifying the lies she once told herself.

While Westover makes it clear that nobody's truth is ever definitive, she emphasizes the importance of telling her version of it. No longer the passive recipient of other peoples' truths, she is determined to take ownership of her story – as both an act of self-assertion and a kind of therapy. The result is an extraordinary memoir which surely deserves to become a classic.

CHARACTERS

Tara Westover

Due to the autobiographical nature of *Educated*, readers get to know two different versions of Tara: the character (who changes as the narrative develops) and the author, (who writes about her experiences retrospectively). These viewpoints differ dramatically at the beginning of Tara's story but merge as the memoir goes on.

In Part One, Westover recounts her experiences from the age of five until the time she leaves Buck's Peak for Brigham Young University. In this section, she occasionally moderates the views of her childhood self with her retrospective wisdom as an adult. After her mother is badly injured in a car accident, for example, she describes calling her "Raccoon Eyes", adding that she now knows this to be a medical term for a symptom of brain injury. On the whole, however, readers are presented with Tara's thoughts and views as a child. This perspective powerfully conveys the way the beliefs of her family shape her.

One of seven children, Tara has no official identity as she does not possess a birth certificate and her parents are unsure of her date of birth. Born at home, she has never seen a doctor or been to school. Raised to think of this as the norm, Tara does not appreciate how unusual her family's lifestyle is. Accepting her father's view of the world, she believes that school is a brainwashing tool of the government, pharmaceuticals are poison and that the end of the world is imminent. Terrified by her father's story about the Ruby Ridge siege, she also believes that her family is in danger from the Feds.

During her early years, Tara has no reason to question the assumption that she will follow in her mother's footsteps. This would mean marrying a devout Mormon, having children and becoming an unofficial midwife. As she grows older, however, certain influences begin to gently tug Tara in another direction. When she begins babysitting (largely to avoid working in the scrapyard), she takes piano lessons from her employer, Mary. At Mary's suggestion, she also begins going to dance class – an experience which proves to be her first lesson in "learning to belong".

Tara's feelings about her dance class mark the beginning of a personal conflict that will plague her for years. While her desire to perform and express herself is strong, the opinions that she absorbs from her father are stronger. This means she feels shame at exposing her body, even when wearing a knee-length T-shirt over her leotard. In the end, her father puts a halt to the classes when he sees the 'immodest' costumes. Tara then finds a new means of self-expression when she has singing lessons and begins to perform in public. It is at this point that she realizes she enjoys her voice being heard. This is a significant discovery for, at home, her voice is drowned out by the rest of her family.

Another important influence on Tara at this stage is her brother Tyler. Nurturing his sister's love of music, he also boosts her self-esteem by treating her as a serious and intelligent person. As a result, Tara feels "transformed" in his presence, realizing she has potential beyond the rest of her family's expectations. It is Tyler who opens up the possibility of an alternative future for Tara by going to college and encouraging his sister to follow in his footsteps. Although Tara has difficulties imagining a different future to the one mapped out for her, Tyler's suggestion that she could study music and become the director of the church choir offers an option that seems just about feasible.

Unfortunately, Tyler's departure to college is followed by the return of another brother: Shawn. While Shawn takes a special interest in his sister and Tara bonds with him, the relationship is to prove devastating to her self-esteem, undoing much of the good work undertaken by Tyler.

Tara feels drawn to Shawn as he seems to offer the protective qualities that are glaringly absent in her father. This impression is initially confirmed when Shawn saves Tara from falling off her runaway horse. Unlike Tyler, however, who is consistent in his support, Shawn alternates kindnesses with cruelties. When Tara reaches adolescence and is at her most vulnerable, Shawn's physical and verbal abuse of her comes to a head. Her brother's repeated assertions that she is unchaste (combined with her father's lectures on immodesty) prompt great anxiety as Tara crosses the threshold of womanhood. As a result, she becomes overwhelmed by self-loathing, believing "There was something impure in the fact of my being."

Despite her inner conflict, we begin to see Tara taking important steps towards agency in this section of her memoir. In the face of Gene's disapproval and his attempts to sabotage her plans, she studies for the ACT and is eventually rewarded with a place at Brigham Young University. She also opposes her father's will on a couple of other occasions – rolling her T-shirt sleeves back up when he pulls them down and defying Gene's instructions by taking Shawn to the hospital after a motorcycle accident. This marks the beginning of Tara's realization that she has a mind independent of her father's.

In Part Two of *Educated*, Westover describes her time as an undergraduate at BYU and Cambridge. During this period, Tara experiences a steep learning curve in more ways than one. Lectures at BYU bring home the vast gaps in her knowledge – illustrated in the fact that she has never heard of the Holocaust. Meanwhile, interaction with fellow students emphasizes how different the Westovers' beliefs are from those of almost everyone she meets. Gradually, Tara's first proper interaction with the outside world expands her mind, and she starts to question some of the beliefs she has absorbed from her family. Reading feminist literature gives her a vocabulary to identify the limiting and misogynist ideas about women shared by her father and Shawn. Learning about the history of the civil rights movement also makes her aware of her family's casually racist use of language.

Although developing ideas of her own, Tara still finds herself restricted by inner voices spouting the beliefs of her family. For a long time, she keeps her fellow students at arm's length, disapproving of their lack of devoutness. She also pushes Charles away, haunted by Shawn's slurs on her character. This situation is not helped by her repeated returns to Buck's Peak where she loses the advantage of geographical distance and reverts to her childhood self.

Tara demonstrates that she has quite literally internalized her father's voice in an exchange with Charles. When he asks if she is angry with her parents for failing to send her to school, she instinctively shouts, "It was an advantage!" Although deep-down, Tara knows that this is nonsense, she explains, "It was like hearing a phrase from a catchy song: I couldn't stop myself from reciting the next line." So loud are her family's voices that they drown out both her own beliefs and the more measured opinions of friends and advisors. This is again proved at Cambridge, where Tara still feels that Shawn's baseless insults ring truer than the praise she earns from the university's eminent professors.

During the battle between forming new opinions and reverting to those of her family, Tara experiences a couple of major turning points. After Shawn assaults and publicly humiliates her in a parking lot, she writes a truthful account of his behaviour in her journal for the first time, offering no excuses on her brother's behalf. Later, when she returns to BYU and receives an apologetic email from Shawn, she backtracks, revising her journal with a note to say the incident was a "misunderstanding". Significantly, however, Tara does not cross out the first entry, leaving both versions to stand. This marks her first tentative step towards acknowledging that she does not have to accept the narrative her family present her with. Similarly, after discovering the truth about the Ruby Ridge siege, Tara furiously confronts her father, accusing him of frightening his family with a false account of events. Returning to university she decides that she wants no further contact with Gene and, for the first time, does not return to her childhood home for the summer holidays. Her resolve evaporates, however, when her father has a terrible accident. Thinking he might die, she is drawn back to Buck's Peak.

Although her family is her Achille's heel, Tara demonstrates great tenacity and determination while pursuing her education. As well as overcoming the gaps in her knowledge, she faces considerable financial difficulties. Already working in a diner, she takes a second job as a cleaner to stay at college and studies through the night to secure a partial scholarship. Westover makes it clear, however, that her path would have been easier if she had been able to accept the help of others. While her housemate Robin and the bishop of her church fall over themselves to offer her assistance, pride prevents Tara from taking it. Her financial problems (and dental pain) are finally solved when she reluctantly applies for a government grant – despite still half-believing her father's claim that they are a blackmailing tool of the Illuminati. On receiving the grant, Tara realizes that the money gives her the luxury of integrity. Armed with independent finances, she will never again be manipulated into working for her father. This knowledge proves to be a liberation and Tara begins to open up to other people. As she does so, she discovers that friendship offers the kind of support that she has rarely received from her parents.

Part Three brings Westover's narrative close to the present day and painfully recounts her mental breakdown. During Tara's emotional crisis, she stops working and socializing, and almost fails her PhD. At this point, she comes close to throwing away everything she has worked so hard for. Tara's great turmoil comes from the realization that her new self is incompatible with maintaining a relationship with her parents. As a result, she believes that the cost of her education has been too great.

Tara's final rift with her parents occurs over her insistence on confronting Shawn's abusive behaviour. While Gene and Faye wish to gloss over the subject, Tara makes their lives uncomfortable by refusing to go along with the charade. This leads to a face-to-face confrontation with Shawn in which he presents her with a bloodied knife and advises her to use it on herself. At this moment, Tara experiences a significant shift in her well-practiced response to Shawn's aggression. Placating her brother by claiming there has been a misunderstanding, she allows him to hug her in a gesture of reconciliation. On this occasion, however, Tara does so purely out of self-preservation. Although acting the part of her younger, compliant self, her reaction is a pretence. For Tara, this is the point of no return for her relationship with Shawn.

Tara's most crucial moment of self-determination comes when Gene and Faye arrive at Harvard, determined to exorcise her of evil. Despite her parents' campaign to turn her other siblings against her, Tara still craves reconciliation with them and plans to agree to the ritual. When the time arrives, however, she cannot succumb to her father's will. Having striven so hard to achieve independence of thought, Tara realizes that she is not prepared to "lose custody" of her mind.

Gene Westover

As a child – and well into adulthood – Tara's life is dominated by the beliefs of her father. Gene's obsessions are diverse in their scope, spanning religious extremism, survivalism and paranoid delusions about the American government. All these beliefs, however, share one thing in common: a desire for control. As a self-styled Mormon prophet, Gene directs and passes judgement upon his family's behaviour, almost as if he were God himself. Meanwhile, his determination to fly under the radar of the government provides him with a sense of agency. Finally, his attraction to survivalism (a popular movement among disenfranchised American males) allows him to believe that, even when the apocalypse cometh, he will be one of the few who is adequately prepared for it.

As one of the youngest Westover siblings, Tara bears the full brunt of her father's zealotry which is in full flow by the time she is six. Growing up fearing the shadowy presence of the government and anticipating the end of the world, she is also deprived of a formal education and social interaction with her peers. She knows from her older siblings, however, that Gene was a very different parent to them in their formative years. Less anxious and more fun-loving, he allowed his eldest sons to go to school for several years before rejecting the education system.

Trying to pinpoint when her father's unconventional streak turned into extremism, Tara sees his reaction to the 1992 Ruby Ridge siege as a turning point. According to Gene, during this siege, the FBI gunned down an entire family in response to their decision to homeschool their children. Years later, however, Tara discovers significant inaccuracies in her father's account. Initially, Tara assumes her father deliberately lied to her about the siege. It is only when she remembers Gene's genuine anxiety at the time that she realizes his story reflected his own warped interpretation of events. In his eyes, the siege "ceased to be a story about someone else", instead becoming "a story about *him*."

Gene's interpretation of Ruby Ridge clearly reflects a viewpoint that is distorted by paranoia and a persecution complex and, when Tara studies psychology at college, she learns that these are two classic symptoms of bipolar disorder. Discovering that other symptoms include "depression, mania … euphoria, delusions of grandeur", she realizes that they describe her father's character traits.

If Gene has bipolar disorder, as Tara suspects, it raises the question of how far he can be held responsible for his behaviour.

This is little consolation for his family, however, who face danger as a result of Gene's actions on a daily basis. Every one of Gene's family suffers serious injuries as a direct result of his recklessness – whether from his dangerous working methods in the scrapyard or his habit of driving in treacherous conditions. Here we see considerable irony in Gene's attitudes for while he claims to want to protect his children from the corruption of the world, he lacks the basic parental instinct to keep them safe.

Perhaps more damaging to Tara than the physical danger is the psychological impact of her father's_misogynistic beliefs about women. As well as having rigid ideas about a woman's place in society, Gene associates female sexuality with sinfulness, lecturing the female members of the family on how to avoid provoking temptation in men. His extreme views are most shockingly illustrated when he claims to have observed "indecent habits" in Audrey's daughters who are age six and under. In the face of Gene's contempt for most women, it is almost inevitable that his daughters will grow up with a sense of self-loathing.

Although her father's idiosyncrasies make her life a misery, Westover cannot help but see the funny side of some of his behaviour – at least in retrospect. Her comparison of Gene to Don Quixote sums up the absurd nature of some of his assertions and beliefs. In Cervantes' comic novel, the eponymous hero is completely delusional, embarking on a series of pointless quests and battles. The famous scene where he attacks a group of windmills believing them to be waving giants, has much in common with Gene's constant battle against imaginary foes. Meanwhile, Tara and the rest of her family are left in the position of Sancho (Quixote's squire), who fails to talk any sense into his master and is often left facing the consequences of his antics. In one scene, Westover brilliantly captures her father's delusional state when she describes him burying a tank of fuel in the ground (in preparation for the end of the world) while whistling "I Feel Pretty". In another, she describes Gene's indignation when, having won a scholarship to Cambridge, Tara fails to tell a newspaper reporter that she was homeschooled. Without further comment, Westover leaves readers to marvel that her father can make this complaint without a trace of irony.

While his irrational actions often speak for themselves, the author is careful not to portray Gene as a cartoonish figure of fun.

Despite her father's delusions, she emphasizes that he is an intelligent man – instinctively understanding trigonometry without ever having been taught it. Westover also expresses compassion for her father and a persisting love. This is nowhere better illustrated than in the description of Gene's dismay when his prediction of the end of the world fails to materialize. Watching him sitting, dejected, in front of the TV, Tara feels great pity for her father and wonders "how God could deny him this."

The author's picture of her father as a destructive force in her life is also balanced by glimpses of an alternative Gene. When Tara first sings in front of the church congregation, she sees a completely different side of her father as he glows with pride and laps up the praise from fellow church-goers. From this point on, Gene actively encourages Tara to sing in public, insisting she should audition for *Annie* – even though this means she may mix with corrupting influences at Worm Creek Opera House. Gene continues to be Tara's biggest fan, always ensuring he has a front row ticket. During her performances, he seems to rise above his urge to isolate his daughter from society and actively want her "voice to be heard." This is one of the great contradictions of Gene's personality for, while his behaviour at home controls and silences Tara, here he sheds this impulse to take pleasure in his daughter's self-expression. In these moments, we see the father Gene might be if he were not overwhelmed by obsessions and paranoia.

Tara also sees a different side to her father as he recuperates from his life-threatening burns. Practicing what he preaches, Gene refuses conventional medicine for his injuries and becomes completely reliant on the ministrations of the women in the family. Gene's new, subservient role is compounded by the fact that his throat injuries make speech painful. Thus restricted, he becomes a listener instead of a lecturer and begins to show an interest in Tara's life at university. For his daughter, this feels like a fresh start.

Unfortunately for Tara, her new, more reflective father evaporates with his recuperation. If anything, Gene's survival of such terrible injuries only strengthens his belief that he has been chosen by God. Following his recovery, Gene's religious mania intensifies and, once again, he comes to see himself as an infallible Christ-like figure. His relationship with Tara reaches the final breaking point when he continues to deny that Shawn is a violent bully and accuses his daughter of troublemaking.

Gene's outlandish claims and denials seem to be the result of a deep-seated shame at his inability to handle Shawn's behaviour. When Tara draws attention to Shawn's actions, she brings to light her father's failures. This leads to one of the most shocking scenes in the book, where Gene seems to take the decision to sacrifice his daughter to Shawn. By calling Shawn and telling him of his sister's accusations, Gene leaves Tara wide open to her brother's unpredictable violence. Even after his son threatens Tara with a knife, he continues to insist that Shawn has been 'saved' and that his daughter needs to be exorcised of evil. Unable to accept this poisoned chalice, Tara has no option but to give up on her relationship with her troubled father.

Faye Westover

In terms of character, Faye Westover is difficult to pin down. While Gene's moods are erratic, he is at least predictable in the themes of his paranoias and obsessions. Faye, meanwhile, presents an inconsistent face to the world, making her real opinions impossible to second guess. On the one hand, she is a subservient wife who allows her family to be dominated by her husband's whims. On the other, she is a remarkable healer and a formidable businesswoman. In her portrait of her mother, Westover tries to work out which is the real Faye, but the results are inconclusive. What is clear is the unsettling lack of certainty she felt in her mother's presence.

At the beginning of *Educated*, Faye's identity is rooted in her role as an obedient wife and mother to seven children. Going along with her husband's unconventional lifestyle choices, she shows little sign of passionately agreeing or disagreeing with them. Tara observes a change in her mother when she becomes an assistant to the self-appointed midwife of the area. Pushed into the position by her husband, Faye initially finds its demands overwhelming. As time goes on, however, she gains confidence and Tara notices that her mother's "weightless quality" transforms into self-assurance. When the midwife leaves the area, Faye takes over the role – one which comes with considerable risks. Not only is Faye responsible for the lives of mothers and their babies but she is also at risk of manslaughter charges if a birth goes wrong. Watching her mother at work, Tara sees "the secret strength of her" for the first time.

Faye's role as a midwife gives her a new confidence in her own abilities. She gives up wearing make-up and stops apologizing for her unadorned appearance, indicating that she feels she has a right to be taken seriously just as she is. The money she earns also shifts the balance of power in her marriage, enabling her to have a phone installed without consulting her husband. In professional terms, this self-belief goes on to become unshakable, causing her to make the astounding claim that she can prevent heart attacks and cure cancer. As her reputation as a healer grows (largely from treating her family's horrific injuries), she builds up a hugely successful company which employs most of her family and many locals.

Despite her impressive achievements and increased sense of self-belief, Faye continues to allow Gene to dictate almost every aspect of family life. Her failure to stand up to her husband is perhaps most shockingly illustrated on the occasions when Gene insists on driving home from Arizona through the night. The first time, she pays a high price for her silence when she suffers a brain injury in the inevitable accident. In the aftermath, she is plagued by migraines and problems with her memory. Nevertheless, the next time Gene makes the same suggestion she says nothing and, once again, they crash.

At times, Faye seems an inattentive parent. When she applies for retrospective birth certificates for her children it becomes clear that she is unsure of Tara's birthdate and cannot even remember what month Luke was born in. There is also the incident where she agrees with Gene that sixteen-year-old Tara should move out, as she is under the impression her daughter is twenty, or possibly even older. In other moments, however, she shows herself to be alert and receptive to her children's needs. When Tara requires a costume for her dance classes, Faye drives forty miles to buy a leotard, tights and jazz shoes while urging her daughter to keep them hidden from Gene. She also pays for a voice teacher for Tara when her husband prohibits the dance lessons. Most surprisingly of all, when Tara is about to give up her plan to go to Brigham Young University, she insists that her daughter must, on no account, do so.

While we see glimpses of a woman who thinks and acts independently of her husband, Faye never stands up for her opinions. Moments after telling Tara that she must go to college, she nods and murmurs "in agreement" when Gene begins ranting about the evils of the academic world. Similarly, when Gene hits the roof over Tara's dance recital costume, she claims to share her husband's indignation – despite having agreed on the costume, in advance, with Tara's dance teacher.

Faye's placatory personality does not just extend to trying to please her husband. She is also shown to lie to her children in an effort to appease them. This character trait is most vividly illustrated when Audrey and Tara approach her about Shawn's abusive behaviour. Acknowledging the truth of their claims, Faye expresses remorse at her failure to protect her daughters. Promising to speak to Gene and make him take action, she also confirms, for the first time that she believes her husband has bipolar disorder and refers to the disease's destructive impact on the family. Surprised at her mother's frank admission of culpability, Tara sees this moment as a real breakthrough in their relationship. Later, however, she discovers that her mother lied when she claimed to have raised the issue of Shawn with Gene. In retrospect, she wonders if "my mother, who had always reflected so perfectly the will of my father, had that night merely been reflecting mine."

Any remaining faith that Tara has in her mother is dashed when Shawn threatens her with the bloodied knife he used to kill his dog. Faye not only fails to stand up for her daughter but also begins the process of turning other family members against Tara, claiming that her story about Shawn is a fantasy. Taken aback by her mother's duplicity, it is little wonder that Tara begins to question her own perception of events.

While Tara eventually ceases contact with her father, she hopes to maintain some kind of relationship with her mother. Faye, however, indignantly refuses to meet unless Gene is also invited. Having already distanced herself from her parents and siblings through her loyalty to Gene, Faye adds her daughter to the string of discarded relatives.

Shawn Westover

Tara's brother, Shawn, is absent from the earlier chapters of *Educated* as he left Buck's Peak when Tara was young. His bid for independence clearly goes awry, however, and he returns to his parents' home when Tara is fourteen years old.

Tara barely remembers Shawn but has heard local rumours that he is "trouble, a bully, a bad egg". The tone of her future relationship with him is set in an incident shortly after Shawn's return. Still suffering from a frozen neck after the family's most recent car accident, Tara is completely unprepared when Shawn sneaks up behind her and violently wrenches her head, making it crack. She collapses from the pain but soon realizes her frozen neck is cured. This "violent, compassionate act" sums up Shawn's attitude towards Tara: a bizarre mixture of tenderness on one hand and cruelty on the other.

Throughout Westover's memoir, there are incidents illustrating Shawn's capacity for generosity and kindness. He drives Tara to rehearsals, teaches her martial arts and gives her money when she is struggling to finance her studies. He also shows more concern over Tara's safety than her parents – saving her when her horse runs wild and protesting when his father asks her to use dangerous machinery. As Westover points out, however, Shawn "was never just the one thing." Offsetting these gestures of brotherly affection are just as many incidents of horrific physical and verbal abuse.

Although Westover paints a clear picture of the pattern of Shawn's abusive behaviour, it proves impossible to identify a single cause. With a strong possibility that Gene's mental illness runs in the family, there is a hint of bipolar disorder in Shawn's erratic behaviour and wild mood swings. His naturally volatile temperament may also be exacerbated by the series of head injuries he suffers. What is clear, however, is that a deep-rooted misogyny lies at the heart of Shawn's manipulative and violent treatment of women.

Shawn's contempt for women is illustrated in the power games he plays to assert his control over his girlfriend, Sadie. When Tara is younger, she observes this behaviour in her brother without being its target. Once she begins transforming into a young woman, however, she also becomes the victim of Shawn's verbal cruelties and physical assaults. Shawn's outbursts are often triggered by signs of his sister's emerging sexuality – seeing her applying lip gloss, for example, or checking her appearance in the mirror before meeting Charles. No longer calling Tara "Siddle Lister", he refers to her as "Fish Eyes", "whore" and "slut" – all derogatory terms that Tara has heard him use in relation to Sadie. While Shawn enjoys hurting his sister, often twisting her wrist or grabbing her by the hair, the real purpose of his attacks is humiliation. This is illustrated in the scene where he pins Tara down in a car park, exposing her underwear in public, and in the way his assaults often conclude by shoving his sister's head down the toilet.

Shawn's desire to stop his sister becoming like 'other women' (i.e. a sexual being) is illustrated when, after apologizing to Tara, he presents her with a pearl necklace (a symbol of purity). His fixation with chastity mirrors Gene's preoccupation with the modesty of women but extends further – into an urge to punish and control the women in his life. Westover painfully conveys the way Shawn's behaviour makes her feel ambivalent about becoming a woman and entering into relationships with men. Her brother's insistence that she is essentially "impure" defines her to herself and breeds self-disgust.

There are many jaw-dropping moments in *Educated* but one of the most shocking aspects of the memoir is the way that Shawn's abusive behaviour is facilitated in the Westover household. Shawn wields an inexplicable power over all of his family. His siblings are afraid of him and Faye and Gene turn a blind eye to the abuse he inflicts upon the rest of their children. Worst still, if anyone points out that Shawn's behaviour is unacceptable, they are threatened with ostracism from the family. Without having to be told, the Westover children know that when Shawn is violent or threatening, the incident should be ignored or quickly glossed over.

While Tara's estrangement from her parents happens by degrees, Shawn is at the centre of their final rift. In the end, it is Tara's decision to no longer cover up for Shawn which proves to be the final nail in the coffin. In two terrifying incidents, Shawn reveals just how dangerous he can be after family members dare to tell the truth about his actions. After his sisters broach his abusive behaviour with their parents, he threatens to shoot Audrey and, later, urges Tara to stab herself with the knife he has recently used to kill his own dog. Still, Gene and Faye refuse to acknowledge the truth, coming up with their own revisionist version of events.

Shawn ends his relationship with Tara in a long accusatory email in which he claims that he loved her most out of all of his siblings. While this seems an extraordinary assertion, Westover's description of the strange bond they shared suggests that there is some truth in it. Despite everything Shawn inflicted upon her, Tara still feels a sense of loss at this final severance with her brother.

Tyler Westover

Noticeably different from his siblings, Tyler is like a fish out of water in the Westover household. While the rest of his family revel in rowdy chaos, he likes books, music and peace. Within the dirt and mess of the Westover home, his personal space is an oasis of order.

Although Tara believes she shares the "rowdy" nature of her other brothers, she feels she has the capacity to be someone else when she is with Tyler. It is he who inspires her interest in classical music and books and, most importantly, offers his sister a different vision of herself. This is illustrated when Tyler sees similarities between a description of Mormon ("a sober child, quick to observe") and Tara. Initially, Tara finds this comparison puzzling. Firstly, she knows that in the Mormon faith a woman cannot be a prophet. Secondly, her brother's perception of her as a serious and intelligent person is out of line with her own perception of herself. In time, Tara realizes that Tyler sees in her "a kind of worth" that is "inherent and unshakable." His assertion of her value as a human being is essential in countering the voice of Shawn who repeatedly sexualizes and belittles her.

Despite his stutter and unassuming manner, Tyler possesses great dignity and integrity. Quietly determined to be a scholar, he saves up for a trigonometry textbook and tells his father that he wants to study in the mornings instead of working in the scrapyard – a battle which (to Tara's astonishment) he occasionally wins. When he announces that he is going to college, Tyler remains unswayed by his father's rants about the Illuminati and it becomes clear that nothing will change his mind.

After breaking out of the life expected of him, Tyler urges Tara to do the same. Although she is initially unconvinced that this is a possibility for her, he eventually persuades her to take the ACT and follow him to Brigham Young University.

Tyler becomes an academic high-flier, studying mechanical engineering and going on to earn a doctorate. He also goes on to marry and have children of his own. Despite being the first to truly break away from Buck's Peak, even he struggles to completely cast off the ingrained beliefs of his parents. This is demonstrated when his wife, Stefanie, tells Tara that it took her years to convince him to have their children immunized. A highly-qualified scientist, he still partially believes vaccinations to be a government conspiracy.

When Tara becomes estranged from Faye, Gene and Shawn, she sadly anticipates that Tyler will follow suit. Tyler, however, sees through his mother's clumsy tale about Shawn, the knife and the dog and pledges his support to Tara. Having been the target of Shawn's cruelty when he was younger, Tyler believes his sister's version of events. He also acts as a negotiator, trying to persuade his parents that Tara is not a corrupting influence. He feels he has made progress when Faye claims she has convinced Gene to take action. In the end, however, he faces the same impasse as Tara when both Gene and Shawn threaten to evict him from the family if he mentions the subject again. Standing by his principles, Tyler co-writes a letter with his wife expressing his support for Tara and condemning his parents' unchristian behaviour. Although not completely cast out from the family, his relationship with his father is never the same again.

Luke Westover

The fourth of the five Westover brothers, Luke has a learning disability. Nevertheless, he has a natural affinity for working with animals and the mountain life is in his blood.

When he is seventeen, Luke accidentally sets himself alight, suffering horrific burns to his leg. With no one else around, he is tended to by ten-year-old Tara. Interestingly, however, when Luke recalls the accident later he remembers his father treating the injury – a version of the truth which is perhaps more comforting to him.

While Luke leaves Buck's Peak for a while to drive trucks, he returns with his wife and numerous children to live in a mobile home behind his parents' barn.

Audrey Westover

As soon as Tara's elder sister Audrey turns fifteen she takes several jobs. Her willingness to accept any type of work – flipping burgers, milking cows etc. is a good indication of how eager she is to escape the constraints of life under her father's roof. At nineteen, she marries Benjamin: a farmer she met while waitressing.

Tara sees little of her sister after Audrey leaves home but spends a day with her during a college vacation. Despite never attending school herself, Audrey chooses to homeschool her children, prompting Tara to wonder what she teaches them. She also lives just seven miles away from their parents. Tara realizes that, while they now seem poles apart, her life would have been very similar to Audrey's had she remained in Buck's Peak.

It emerges that the sisters have more in common than Tara imagined when, on her return to college, Audrey emails her. Admitting that Shawn was abusive towards her, Audrey expresses regret that she did not stop the same thing happening to Tara. Going on to confront Faye about Shawn's behaviour (with Tara's support), Audrey extracts a promise from her mother that she will persuade Gene to take action. While Tara is in Europe, however, Audrey clearly gives in to pressure from her parents to back down. In an email to Tara, she reveals that she has followed God's will and forgiven Shawn. Claiming that Tara is a bad influence, she tells her sister never to contact her again.

While Audrey's dramatic change of heart is a huge blow to Tara, it is clear that her parents' machinations become too much for her to bear. This is indicated in an earlier incident when she pleads with Tara not to return to Cambridge as she is afraid of confronting Shawn and her parents alone. While Tara has the benefit of distance from Buck's Peak, Audrey lives in close proximity to her parents and, despite her early bid for independence, is reliant upon them for income. Once she has turned against Tara, she remains in her parents' camp, claiming that her sister is committing a great sin by refusing contact with their father. By succumbing to parental pressures, Audrey continues to represent the path that Tara could so easily have taken.

Richard Westover

Like his siblings, Tara and Tyler, Richard shows a natural affinity for learning. As Tara tries to escape work in the scrapyard to study religion, her youngest brother sneaks into the basement to read an encyclopaedia. Unaware that his son is hiding down there, Gene frequently switches off the basement light. When this happens, Richard continues to read in the dark – so strong is his thirst for knowledge.

While Tara has to fight her father to take the ACT and go to college, Gene later shows a completely different attitude towards Richard, urging him to take the ACT and proclaiming him to be a scientific "genius". This turnabout illustrates Gene's unpredictability as well as his sexist beliefs about appropriate gender roles.

Like Tara, Richard goes on to be academically successful, completing a degree and PhD in chemistry. He also marries and has a son, Donovan. Richard's wife, Kami, is a Mormon but is moderate in her beliefs. Although she politely listens to Faye's herbal advice, she consults doctors and gives birth to her son in hospital.

Observing Richard with his wife and parents, Tara notices how he tries to occupy both worlds and please both sides. While he smiles at Kami when Gene refers to the medical profession as the "minions of Satan", he assumes a serious expression of agreement when his father's gaze falls on him. Tara is, of course, more than familiar with this experience, living one life at university but reverting to her old self when she returns to Buck's Peak.

Tony Westover

When Tara is young, her eldest brother, Tony, drives rigs. Later, he goes on to run his own trucking company in Las Vegas. Tony's business falls victim to the recession, however, and, with a wife and five children to support, he moves back to Buck's Peak to work for Faye and Gene. Although financially dependent upon his parents, Tony remains in touch with Tara after the rift.

Grandma-down-the-hill

While Gene chooses to live just a stone's throw away from his parents' house, he has a combative relationship with his mother. Grandma-down-the-hill is the antithesis of Faye. A "force of nature – impatient, aggressive, self-possessed", she presents a formidable figure with her dyed jet-black hair and heavily pencilled eyebrows.

Having lived in Buck's Peak for half a century, Grandma-down-the-hill reveres the mountain's history – an attitude which she passes down to her son. A love of the area is, however, the only thing that she and Gene agree on. During Tara's childhood, her paternal grandmother is the only person to openly mock the absurdity of her son's ideas. When Gene announces his divine revelation on the evils of dairy products, she responds by filling her own fridge with milk and encouraging Tara to sneak over and indulge. She also disapproves of Gene's decision not to send his children to school and shows that she is prepared to defy him when she offers Tara the opportunity to go to school in Arizona – without her son's consent.

While there is humour in her responses to Gene's wild schemes, it becomes clear that Grandma-down-the-hill's biting sarcasm conceals fear for her son and his family. When Gene announces that he intends to drive through the night in a storm, she expresses her incredulity but can do nothing to stop him. Her eventual air of resignation acknowledges that, if he failed to learn his lesson from his previous accident, there is simply no reasoning with him. Readers are, however, left to ponder the anxiety she must experience as her family drive away towards inevitable disaster.

When Gene's mother is diagnosed with bone marrow cancer, her decision to have chemotherapy (as well as accepting herbal treatments from Faye) becomes another source of argument. Gene continues the disagreement even after her death, declaring that if she had trusted in God and the power of Faye's tinctures she would have been spared.

Grandpa-down-the-hill

Gene's father largely fades into the background of Tara's memoir, suggesting that his wife was the driving force of the partnership. The story of how he acquired a dent in his forehead, however, becomes family legend.

According to his version of events, Grandpa-down-the-hill fell off his horse on the mountain, hit his head and then remembered nothing more until his wife found him lying outside their house. Meanwhile, his horse was later found tied up with a distinctive knot only ever used by his master. In all likelihood, the explanation for this mystery is straightforward. Driven by a powerful instinct for survival, Tara's grandfather dragged himself down the mountain in a semi-conscious state, securing his horse out of habit. Tara's parents, however, interpret this story as evidence that angels carried Gene's father down the mountain.

Grandma & Grandpa-over-in-town

Tara's maternal grandparents gain their nicknames as they live in the only town in the county. Although the small town boasts little more than road markings and a grocery store, this is considered cosmopolitan living by the rest of the Westover clan.

As a child, Tara rarely sees her mother's parents as their disapproval of Gene has made relations with their daughter strained. Tara's impressions of her grandparents are built upon her father's disparaging comments about their conventional lifestyle. Sneering at the respectability of their home, Gene dismisses Faye's mother as "frivolous". He also declares the cleanliness of their house to be proof that Tara's grandpa (a former mailman) has never undertaken manly work. Tara briefly questions this assessment of her grandparents when she wonders if there might be some validity to her grandmother's lecture on handwashing after using the bathroom. Back in the presence of her father, however, she quickly reverts to his viewpoint.

As the memoir progresses, Tara comes to a much better understanding of who her grandmother was, particularly when she learns her backstory. Growing up in a strict Mormon community, with an alcoholic for a father, Tara's grandmother was a social outcast. Scarred by this experience, she then devoted her life to ensuring that her daughters would never be treated as pariahs. Buying a house with a white picket fence, she used her skills as a seamstress to dress her children in beautiful clothes. It was this very fixation with respectability, however, that Faye kicked against by marrying Gene.

Sadly, Tara only learns the truth from her aunts and uncles once her grandmother dies of Alzheimer's. Then she appreciates that her Grandma's "polite smile" concealed the grief of doing her best for her daughter, only to lose her. Too late, Tara realizes that her maternal grandmother was probably one of the few people to understand the divisive impact of Gene's extremist views. While Tara misses out on the opportunity to build a relationship with her grandmother, her memoir gives her the opportunity to write the truth about her. This seems a particularly fitting tribute to the woman who bought Tara her first journal as a child.

Anna Mathea

Tara's great-great-grandmother Anna Mathea is presented as a role model to her granddaughter. When Tara discovers that she can sing, Faye tells her that she has inherited her voice from her Norwegian ancestor. Tara, however, becomes increasingly uneasy about following in her great-great-grandmother's footsteps.

While Gene and Faye revere her religious devotion, Tara thinks of her great-great-grandmother's history with sadness. After converting her parents to Mormonism, she was left in Norway while her mother and father followed God's call to America. Anna became engaged but gave up her fiancé to join her parents in America when her mother fell seriously ill. On her mother's death, she was married off to a rich farmer, becoming a second wife. After having twins, however, Anna moved back with her father to protect her children from her husband's jealous first wife. Nevertheless, only one of her twins survived.

Anna Mathea's fate is a reminder of the self-sacrifice required of Mormon women. Thinking about her great-great-grandmother, Tara realizes that she never wants to become one of multiple wives – even in the afterlife.

Aunt Angie

When costumes are needed for Tara's role as Annie, Faye drives to every charity shop in the district before she resorts to asking for her sister's help. Despite rarely seeing Faye since her marriage to Gene, Angie is welcoming to her sister and niece and finds suitable dresses for Tara to wear.

Years later, Faye enlists Angie for her essential oils business but Gene fires her, accusing his sister-in-law of having him placed on a terrorist watch list. This illustrates Gene's divisive impact upon his wife's relationship with her family. Estranged from her parents at the time of her grandmother's funeral, Tara chooses to stay with Angie, who becomes her ally.

Aunt Debbie

Debbie is another sister largely ignored by Faye once she has married Gene. Nevertheless, she is a supportive aunt to her nieces and nephews. During his first year at Brigham Young University, Tyler lives with Aunt Debbie and her home becomes a quiet meeting place when he coaches Tara in trigonometry. When Tara has difficulty getting a passport, it is Debbie who ensures her niece can go to Cambridge by swearing an affidavit confirming her identity.

Although Tara hardly knows Debbie during her early years, her aunt becomes increasingly important to her. Estranged from her parents and some of her siblings, Tara claims her as part of her new family.

Charles

When Tara is starring as Annie at the Worm Creek Opera House she meets Charles – a boy of a similar age. Charles goes on to become Tara's "first friend from that other world, the one my father had tried to protect me from." Far from a corrupting influence, he is to prove a positive force in Tara's life.

While Charles's family are also Mormons, they do not share Gene's suspicion of government institutions. Tara is surprised to learn that Charles attends the local high school and his family consult doctors when they are sick. It is through her interactions with Charles that Tara begins to realize her own family's values are by no means the norm.

When Tara is a teenager she is attracted to Charles, but he is in love with Sadie. This makes him the focus of Shawn's hostility in more ways than one. Shawn's dislike of seeing his girlfriend socializing with Charles is exacerbated by Tara's interest in him.

Tara's friendship with Charles finally turns into something like romance when she returns for the summer from BYU. While they are dating, she does her best to keep her family and Charles in two separate worlds. They disastrously collide, however, when Charles comes over for Thanksgiving dinner and is treated to a front-row view of Shawn's abusive behaviour. Stunned, he witnesses Shawn pin his sister to the floor, drag her to the bathroom by the hair and shove her head in the toilet. Meanwhile, Tara does her best to pretend that this is normal family high jinks. In the aftermath, Charles tries to discuss the incident with Tara, but she pushes him away, resenting him for having witnessed her humiliation. Eventually, Charles regretfully tells Tara that he loves her but only she is capable of saving herself. In retrospect, Tara bitterly regrets the way she vented her anger at Charles, realizing that he was a "bewildered bystander who'd only ever helped me." Perhaps one of the saddest elements of her memoir is the way she rejects Charles due to her lack of self-esteem.

Later, when Tara is at Harvard, she gets back in touch with Charles via an Internet chat room. He reveals that he never graduated from college as his wife became sick after their son was born. Instead, he went to work on the oil rigs to pay their medical bills. During their exchanges, Tara confides in Charles about the rift with her family. Once again, he provides wise advice by suggesting she should "just let them go".

Sadie

When Shawn begins taking his sister to Worm Creek Opera House, Sadie spots Tara's brother and sets her sights on him. The child of divorcing parents, and still in high school, she becomes a tragically vulnerable target for Shawn's cruelty. Labelling her "Fish Eyes" (i.e. beautiful but vacant), Shawn takes pleasure in publicly humiliating Sadie, sending her to buy candy and then claiming she has bought the wrong kind. His treatment of her turns out to be a forewarning of how he will behave towards Tara when she becomes a young woman.

Although she has an alternative suitor waiting in the wings (in the shape of the thoroughly decent Charles), Sadie is continually drawn back to Shawn and even tells boys not to speak to her in case it provokes her boyfriend's displeasure. Her inability to escape Shawn's thrall is later echoed in Tara's behaviour when she continues to spend time alone with him, despite fearing he will hurt her.

Emily

When Shawn begins dating Emily, he is twenty-eight, while she is still a senior in high school. Impressionable and delicately built, she possesses the kind of "compliant" nature that Shawn looks for in a partner. When Tara first meets Emily, she is dismayed to see that her brother controls and humiliates her – just as he did with his previous girlfriend, Sadie.

Now armed with the intellectual tools to identify their relationship as abusive, Tara broaches the subject of Shawn's violent and manipulative behaviour with Emily. While Emily admits that she is scared of Shawn, she clams up when Tara suggests that she should not marry him.

In the period leading up to Shawn's wedding, Tara feels that she should do something to prevent the marriage. Her urge to intervene reflects a desire to protect Emily from the abuse that she also suffered at his hands (and that no one else protected her from). In the end, she takes no action but is haunted by the fear that Emily is in serious danger.

Tara's forebodings prove to be well-founded as Emily suffers greatly during her marriage to Shawn. Continuing to work for Faye's mother during a difficult pregnancy, she gives birth to her son, Peter, after only twenty-six weeks. Later, after she becomes pregnant again, with a daughter, Emily nearly dies during a home birth, attended to by her mother-in-law. Gene and Faye choose to interpret both births as miracles orchestrated by God. For Tara, however, these near-misses illustrate a cavalier attitude (on the part of both her brother and her parents) to Emily's welfare.

Shawn's cruel treatment of his wife is illustrated when, one snowy night, she appears at the Westovers' house wearing no coat or shoes. Throwing her out of their trailer turns out to be Shawn's way of punishing his wife for buying the wrong crackers for their son. Faced with Emily's distress, Tara and the rest of the Westover family are left in no doubt that Shawn is an abusive husband. To her shame, however, Tara falls back into her compliant childhood role, telling Richard and his wife, Kami, that they should leave Gene to deal with the situation. Embarrassed that Kami has witnessed the scene, Tara tries to gloss over it – just as she did as a teenager when Charles witnessed Shawn's assault of her. Later, she bitterly regrets failing to call the police.

Erin

When her parents remain in denial about Shawn's dangerous tendencies, Tara begins to doubt her own recollection of events. Seeking clarity, she writes to Shawn's former girlfriend, Erin. Erin replies, assuring Tara that her memories of Shawn's rages and verbal abuse are accurate, as she was also the victim of them. In her letter, she recounts an incident when Shawn almost killed her by slamming her head against a wall.

Erin's letter briefly assures Tara of her sanity until she begins to wonder if Shawn's ex-girlfriend could also be mad. This possibility is ruled out when she meets Erin's cousin who confirms that, if her grandfather had not intervened, Shawn would almost certainly have killed Erin.

When Tara returns to Buck's Peak anticipating a reconciliation with her family, she comes across an email from Faye to Erin claiming that, while Shawn has been 'saved', Tara remains the dangerous element in their family. The email reminds Tara that her mother cannot be trusted.

Judy

When her mother becomes an assistant to the local midwife, Tara is struck by how different the two women are. Although Judy has no medical qualifications she is "a midwife entirely by the power of her own say-so". Impressively authoritative with a no-nonsense manner, Judy juggles midwifery and caring for eleven children.

Tara's mother initially feels unequal to her role as Judy's assistant. As she becomes more experienced, however, she absorbs not only her mentor's knowledge but also her air of authority. By the time Judy announces that she is leaving the area, Faye is ready to step into the midwife's shoes.

Maria

By the age of nine, Judy's daughter, Maria, has witnessed many births. With a baby permanently attached to her hip, she has a knowledgeable air that young Tara aspires to.

Mary

When Tara is eleven, she babysits the children of a local woman named Mary. After hearing Mary's beautiful piano playing in church, Tara asks for music lessons in lieu of payment. Guessing that Tara has no friends, Mary suggests that she also enrols in the dance classes run by her sister, Caroline.

Caroline Moyle

Welcoming Tara to her dance class, Caroline does her best to ensure that her new pupil does not feel excluded. After Tara turns up for her first class in jeans and steel-toed boots, Caroline shows considerable persuasive skills by convincing Faye that her daughter needs a leotard and dance shoes. Later, when Faye tells Caroline that the costume for a recital is too immodest, the dance teacher comes up with new outfits for the girls, dowdy enough for even Faye to approve.

Caroline and her sister Mary are both examples of people who offer support and kindness to Tara during her early years. Spotting her social isolation, they try to introduce her to 'normality'.

Myrna & Jay Moyle

Caroline's parents are the owners of the local gas station - Papa Jay's. Relative newcomers to the area, the Moyles propose various improvements (including limiting the number of dogs a family can own). This causes Gene to scathingly accuse them of "Californian socialism".

Shannon & Mary

On moving into college accommodation, Tara expects her Mormon housemates to be similarly modest and devout. This assumption is shattered when she meets Shannon and Mary. While, at this point, Tara still wears men's jeans and shirts, Shannon parades around in a strappy top and pyjama bottoms with 'Juicy' written across the rear. Meanwhile, Mary drinks Diet Coke and violates the Sabbath by going grocery shopping. Accustomed to the religious extremism of her father, Tara struggles to believe that her housemates are church-going Mormons. She soon discovers, however, that Shannon and Mary's conduct is the norm at BYU and it is her own beliefs that are out of step with everyone else. Writing about her reaction to her housemates in retrospect, Westover makes fun of her own horrified naivety.

Vanessa

When Tara starts studying at BYU she is drawn to Vanessa as she seems more like-minded and devout than the other students. Vanessa is, at first, a guiding influence on Tara, pointing out that her 'joke' about the Holocaust was "inappropriate". Her patience is pushed to the limit, however, when Tara reveals she did not realize they were expected to read their textbooks. From this point, Vanessa avoids Tara, but her study tips prove invaluable to her former friend's academic success.

Robin

Robin is the second friend Tara makes at BYU and their friendship proves to be an enduring one. On meeting Tara, Robin intuits that her housemate's odd behaviour stems from "ignorance, not intention". She makes it her job to guide Tara in societal norms, helping her to get along with others. Thanks to Robin, Tara learns to clean up after herself and starts washing her hands after using the bathroom.

Endlessly kind and supportive, Robin comforts Tara when she is ill, offers to take her to a doctor, suggests counselling, and forces her friend to post her grant application. She is a shining example of how friends can sometimes offer positive qualities significantly lacking in one's own family.

The Bishop

When Tara turns down two potential suitors from her church she gains a reputation for being set against marriage. For this reason, she is called to see the bishop (the spiritual leader of her church). Tara is surprised to find the bishop kindly and easy to confide in and she begins to visit him every Sunday. The bishop's manner provides a refreshing contrast to that of Tara's father. Although he holds a patriarchal role, he wears his power lightly, seeking to help rather than control.

The bishop proves to be an invaluable source of support throughout Tara's struggles, offering emotional and practical guidance. Recognizing the toxic impact of Tara's family, he urges her not to go home during the holidays, suggesting that the church could pay her rent. He also offers to pay for her root canal work and informs Tara that she should be eligible for a government grant. True to character, Tara turns down these offers out of pride but is finally persuaded to apply for the grant that allows her to continue with her studies.

Dr. Kerry

When Tara realizes that she wants to drop music to study geography, politics and history, she goes to see Dr. Kerry: the professor of her Jewish history class at BYU. Looking for guidance on whether these 'masculine' disciplines are really appropriate for a woman, she is surprised when Dr. Kerry recommends a study abroad program at Cambridge. Although the University of Cambridge initially rejects Tara's application, Dr. Kerry argues her case. He also tries to persuade Tara of her worth when she suffers from imposter's syndrome at Cambridge.

Professor Steinberg

At Trinity College, Cambridge, Tara is assigned Professor Steinberg as her supervisor. An expert on the Holocaust, he is delighted to discover Tara's lack of formal education, comparing her to Pygmalion.

When Tara submits her first essay to Steinberg he pronounces that it is one of the best he has read in thirty years of teaching. From that point, he becomes Tara's academic champion, ensuring that she is accepted to the graduate school of her choice.

Drew

Tara begins dating her friend Drew when she is studying at Cambridge and he is the first boyfriend she fully confides in. Towards the end of her memoir, she reveals they have moved into a London flat together.

LOCATION

Tara Westover's education involves not only an expansion of her mind but also of her geographical horizons. During her memoir, she travels to a number of different places. Each of them has an impact on determining the person she is to become.

Buck's Peak

Tara grows up in Idaho in a house that stands in the shadow of a mountain. A rural farming community, Buck's Peak is miles from the nearest town. This geographical isolation means that, during her childhood, Tara's experiences of the outside world are extremely limited. With little else to compare her family to, she assumes that there is nothing particularly unusual about their unconventional way of life.

Despite the painful emotions she comes to associate with her childhood, Westover depicts the landscape of Buck's Peak with love and a hint of nostalgia. Young Tara's affinity with this vast mountainous landscape makes her feel liberated. It also gives her the sense that the dramas of human life are unimportant in the grand scale of things.

Dominating this landscape is the mountain, known to the Westovers as "the Indian Princess." While she is a dangerous place for the unwary, Tara thinks of the Indian Princess as a kind of guardian angel to her family. When away from Buck's Peak, she feels as if the Princess is calling her back. Tara's repeated returns to her childhood home seem to be an answer not only to the duties of family but also to the siren call of the mountain.

In direct contrast to the wild beauty of the mountain is the eyesore that is Gene's scrapyard. The primary source of family income when Tara is young, the yard is a jungle of wrecked cars, trucks, corrugated metal and leaking batteries.

As a small child, Tara has fun "plundering" the scrapyard and playing on the old railway car. Once she turns ten, however, she is expected to work in the yard and suddenly remembers the past injuries suffered by her brothers. At this point, her perception of the junkyard changes from a "childhood playground" to a dangerous and "hostile" environment. Terrified, she prays to the angels to protect her as she is working. Tara's fears for her safety are more than justified by Gene's dangerous working methods and the fact that she has never had a tetanus shot.

For Tara, working in the junkyard involves a loss of innocence and a new awareness of the harsh realities of her future. Her recent discovery of the joy of music is subsumed by the deafening sounds of her workplace: "the jingle of corrugated tin, the short tap of copper wire, the thunder of iron."

As the junkyard is Gene's domain, it is also the location where he exerts the most control over his offspring. Forcing them to work there from a young age, he does all he can to ensure that they stay and submit to his orders. Some of the fiercest battles of will between Shawn and Gene take place in this territory and, even after Tara leaves for college, her father manipulates her into returning to work there. For this reason, Tara equates working in the scrapyard with falling back into the patterns of her old life and begins to believe that she will never escape this fate.

Although Tara eventually escapes the world of the junkyard, she notes that her father's dominion begins to take over the landscape, marring its beauty: "The rolling hills, once perfect lakes of snow, were dotted with mangled trucks and rusted septic tanks." Gene's damaging impact on the environment neatly reflects the destructive effect of his behaviour on his family.

Grandma-over-in-town's House

The home of Faye's parents provides a startling contrast to the chaos and disorder of the Westover household. With its white picket fence and spotless décor, grandma-over-in-town's house represents the conventional lifestyle that Faye turned her back on when she married Gene.

Tyler, who craves order and calm, is naturally drawn to his grandparents' house. Meanwhile, Gene predictably sneers at its respectability and, for a long time, Tara sees the house through her father's eyes. She does, however, experience a momentary shift in her perception when confronted with the soap in her grandparents' bathroom. As soap plays no part in the lives of the Westovers, Tara cannot help picking up the swan-shaped bar as if it is some exotic curiosity. Although she does not go so far as to wash her hands with it, she admires the soap and briefly considers taking it home. Imagining it in the setting of her parents' house, however, she realizes it would be completely out of place and decides against it. This moment shows Tara briefly considering the attractions of a different, more conventional sort of life. She is then given further food for thought when her grandmother stresses the importance of washing her hands after using the bathroom.

At this point in her life, Tara is not ready to cast off the values of her parents in favour of those of her grandparents. As soon as Gene dismissively tells his mother-in-law that he has taught his children "not to piss on their hands", Westover recounts that "A familiar lens slid over my eyes and Grandma lost whatever strange power she'd had over me an hour before." These issues are to arise again, however, years later, when Tara goes to BYU and her housemates make pointed remarks about her failure to wash her hands. Realizing that her father's values make her a social outcast, Tara eventually sees the value in her grandmother's respectable lifestyle choices.

Worm Creek

After landing the starring role in *Annie*, Tara attends rehearsals at the Opera House in Worm Creek. While Worm Creek is only a small provincial town, it might as well be another planet to Tara who has rarely left Buck's Peak. This marks her first exposure to people from outside her church community and Gene fears that his daughter will be corrupted. In reality, Tara sees little evidence of the "adulterers and fornicators" her father warns her of. The experience does, however, make her realize that her family's values are unusual. Making her first friend in Charles, she begins to envy the normality of his life.

Brigham Young University

While Tara dips her toes into the outside world at Worm Creek, she receives a thorough dunking when she goes to Brigham Young

University in Utah. For many reasons, this proves to be an overwhelming experience for her. Feeling assaulted by the noise of the city, she is also affronted by the behaviour of her fellow students. Initially lulled into a false sense of security by the fact that BYU is a Mormon college, she is shocked to discover that almost everyone is "a gentile" (her father's word for Mormons who are not sufficiently pious). She also discovers the gaping holes in her understanding of the world.

Studying at BYU, Tara feels a disconnect with her surroundings. She misses the presence of the Indian Princess on the skyline and, when she looks out at the Rockies from her bedroom window, she thinks they look "Like paintings." This reflects Tara's sense that, as a student, she is acting a role and her surroundings are like a theatrical backdrop.

As time goes on, and she settles into her studies, Tara's life in Utah begins to feel more authentic – so much so that, when her parents visit, it is their behaviour that seems surreal. Deep-down, however, she remains divided between her life as a scholar and her entirely different existence as the child of her parents. As a result, Tara develops a split identity, reverting to her old role when she returns to Buck's Peak. This division in her sense of self reflects the fact that she knows these two identities are mutually exclusive and cannot be merged into a harmonious whole.

Trinity College, Cambridge

When Tara has a crisis over which subjects to study, her professor at BYU suggests an exchange program at the University of Cambridge, England. Dr. Kerry hopes that the experience will help Tara to recognize her academic potential.

Getting to Cambridge is no mean feat for Tara. Not only does she have to disregard her father's disapproval, but she also has difficulties applying for a passport with her delayed birth certificate. The trip is also a symbolic journey for, in crossing the Atlantic to Europe, she reverses the pilgrimage that her Mormon great-great-grandmother from Norway made to the USA. While her ancestor made the voyage out of religious and familial duty, Tara's journey is one of self-discovery.

Once she arrives at Trinity College, Cambridge, Tara is intimidated by the university's ancient grandeur. Feeling completely out of place in this world of cloisters, pristine lawns and bowler hat-wearing porters, Tara concludes that "Someone like me did not belong at Cambridge."

Tara feels that her fears are confirmed during a tour of one of the chapels. As the group go up on the roof to admire the view, Dr. Kerry notices that, while the other students look unsteady, Tara suddenly looks fearless and completely at home. Tara takes the professor's observation as a further sign that she does not belong there: "I wanted the mind of a scholar, but it seemed that Dr. Kerry saw in me the mind of a roofer." This assumption reflects Tara's insecurities, as the quality that Dr. Kerry really sees in her at this moment is a great inner strength.

While studying at Cambridge, Tara receives confirmation from her professors that she is an exceptional scholar with a bright academic future ahead of her. Despite this affirmation of her abilities, she remains conflicted. Presented with opposing concepts of her identity - the one her professors attribute to her and the one prescribed by Shawn - she is unable to reconcile the two: "Scholar or whore, both couldn't be true. One was a lie."

Tara proves beyond doubt that she belongs at Cambridge when she returns as a graduate student. It is here, thousands of miles away from Buck's Peak, that she eventually begins to turn a corner in shaking off her family's influence. Freeing herself from some of her inner constraints, she embraces feminism, opens up to other people and begins to live a more 'normal' life.

Rome

During her time at Cambridge, Tara gets to see more of Europe's history when she visits Rome with a group of other students. At first, she views the ancient city like a museum, approaching it with awe and reverence. By the times she leaves, however, Rome has become vivid and alive to her.

Harvard

Studying at Cambridge means that, when Tara begins her PhD at Harvard, Massachusetts, she is not overly intimidated by the university's prestige and beauty. Here, she begins to incorporate her own experiences into her academic work by analysing the way in which a person's familial obligations may clash with "their obligations to society as a whole."

Tara's time at Harvard is one of great personal crisis as her conflict with her parents grows into an unhealable rift. Feeling that the price of her education has been the loss of her family, she comes close to throwing away everything she has worked for. Unable to concentrate on her studies, she is in danger of failing her PhD and stops socializing with her friends.

Tara eventually comes through her mental breakdown with the help of the university's counselling service. Resuming her studies, she completes her PhD and becomes Dr. Westover. This academic title confirms her identity as a scholar.

The Bedouin Camp

While undertaking her PhD Tara travels from Harvard to visit Drew in the Middle East. Staying in a Bedouin camp in the desert, she is suddenly struck by how far she has travelled (emotionally and geographically) in the course of her education.

THEMES & SYMBOLISM

THEMES

Education

The overriding theme of Tara Westover's memoir is reflected in its title. Throughout the narrative, the author strives to address two questions: what is an education, and what is its value?

At the beginning of *Educated*, seven-year-old Tara knows that she is different from other children because she does not get on the school bus in the morning. This difference, however, does not trouble her. Well-versed in her father's belief that schools are part of the government's plan to made children "ungodly", she assumes that she is not missing out.

Gene's assertion that education is a scheme to brainwash young people is ironic when we see the way he indoctrinates his children with his own beliefs. He encourages his children to read the books of God for, as Westover observes, they teach her "what to think, not how to think for myself." Other books are considered dangerous.

Gene does his best to convince his offspring that education has no value in the real world. Thus, when Tyler makes the announcement that he is going to college he scornfully replies– "How can you support a wife and children with *books*?" Having always made his living by practical skills, Gene wants his sons to follow in his footsteps.

When Tara is very young, Faye's attitude towards education is markedly different from her husband's. Happy to homeschool her children, she initially believes that she can provide a better education than the state and takes her role as a teacher seriously. Continually interrupted by Gene diverting their children to the scrapyard, however, she eventually gives up and introduces "self-directed" learning. The efficacy of this system is illustrated when Tara boasts to her mother of completing "fifty pages" of work after idly flicking through a textbook.

Tara's view of formal schooling begins to change after Tyler leaves for Brigham Young University. As her brother flourishes at college, Tara begins to suspect that the education system may have its merits. Deciding that she wants to go to school, she plucks up the courage to tell her father. Predictably, however, Gene responds that her wishes are a betrayal of God's will and her family. With this accusation of disloyalty, Gene temporarily silences Tara. For a second time, she finds herself missing out on school from a sense of obligation to her father (the first time being when she fails to accompany her grandparents to Arizona).

While Gene is victorious in this particular battle, he has not won the war against Tara's desire for an education. Urged on by Tyler, she studies for the ACT with a view to following her brother to BYU. Despite her father's transparent attempts to sabotage her studies (on one occasion asking her to water the fruit trees during a rainstorm), Tara develops "the patience to read things I could not yet understand." It is only when she arrives at BYU as a seventeen-year-old, however, that she discovers just how limited her education has been. With scant knowledge of geography, she is initially under the impression that Europe is a country. She has also never heard of the Holocaust and humiliates herself by asking what the word means in class. Confronted with the enormity of just how much she doesn't know, Tara realizes her isolated lifestyle and lack of access to information have prevented her from understanding the world in general. Despite feeling completely out of her depth in her classes, she is seized with a desire to fill those gaps in her understanding. It is this hunger for an overview of the world and how it works that leads her to drop music in favour of history, geography and politics.

In the course of her classes, Tara realizes that her father has not only stood in the way of her education but also fed her with misinformation. After hearing a fellow student mention the Ruby Ridge siege, she researches the incident and discovers that her father misrepresented the facts. Her subsequent fury springs from the fact that, as a child, she believed her father's distorted version of events and this story hugely influenced the way she saw the world. Realizing that the 'truths' delivered by her father cannot necessarily be trusted, she begins to examine them more critically. Separating her own thoughts from her father's proves a lengthy process. Even when she goes on to become a graduate student at Cambridge, Tara struggles to fully embrace the concept of positive liberty – a freedom "from irrational fears and beliefs ... and all other forms of self-coercion."

Tara's education involves more than just an accumulation of academic knowledge. Living with other students, she discovers that much of what was normal in the Westover household is considered strange or unacceptable by her peers. Accustomed to living in a dirty home, Tara annoys her housemates with her failure to do her share of the chores and lack of personal hygiene. Just as she has to learn the correct way to study, she must also learn how to behave in order to get along with others. Slowly she realizes that education is an ongoing life process which also involves making friends and trying new experiences.

Tara's great dilemma in *Educated* is that the more she learns, the more her relationship with her parents deteriorates. This conflict comes to a head in Part Three when she registers for a PhD at Harvard. Having almost reached the heights of academic achievement, Tara begins to resent her education for causing a seemingly unresolvable rift with her family. Her predicament is that the rounded, educated person she has become is incompatible with the Tara her parents insist that she must be in order to remain in their lives.

At the end of her memoir, the author remains distressed at this fracture with her family. Summing up, however, she cannot regret her educational journey. Opening up new horizons, her education has also, most importantly, given her the confidence to trust her own thoughts and voice. It is these thoughts and this voice that she shares with the reader in *Educated*.

Family

As discussed above, Tara Westover's memoir revolves around the conflict between her desire to be educated and her loyalties towards her family. In the end, she has to acknowledge that to achieve the former she must accept the loss of the latter. This is a slow and painful journey, however, and Tara's difficulty in facing this uncomfortable truth powerfully illustrates the pull of family ties.

Early on in *Educated* we see that certain members of Tara's family are detrimental to her wellbeing. Her father's unconventional collection of beliefs warps the way she sees the world. Meanwhile, her sense of self-esteem is worn away by Shawn's abusive behaviour and her parents' failure to protect her.

In choosing an education, Tara takes the first step towards distancing herself from her family, both emotionally and geographically. Going against her father's wishes when she goes to college, she begins to shed some of the deeply ingrained beliefs she has absorbed since childhood. At the same time, she feels guilty about this disloyalty – a conflict which leads her to base her PhD on what happens when an individual's "obligations to their family conflict with *other* obligations - to friends, to society, to themselves".

Despite developing ideas which make her increasingly at odds with her family, Tara still craves the love and approval of her parents. This is illustrated in the heart-breaking scene where Gene and Faye fail to turn up to her graduation dinner despite the fact that she is being presented with the history department's "most outstanding undergraduate" award. Desperate for them to attend her graduation ceremony, Tara apologizes for her former disagreement with her father and assures Gene that he is free to speak his mind to her professors. By the time her parents arrive, the graduation ceremony is almost over, and Tara has spent the day watching her friends being photographed with their proud parents.

Although Tara's relationship with her family becomes increasingly fraught, she repeatedly returns to Buck's Peak in the fragile hope that she can "fix" things. Time and again, she finds that her family will only accommodate her if she reverts to her childhood self. Her hopeless inability to give up on the situation is vividly illustrated when she decides to return to Buck's Peak for Christmas, facing the distinct possibility that Shawn might kill her. In doing so, she ignores Drew's advice and the warnings of her subconscious (expressed in a dream in which she is lying on a gurney and her father is telling the police that she has stabbed herself.) Tara's dream clearly demonstrates that she knows her family is a psychological and physical threat to her. Nevertheless, she goes home anyway. It is only when she discovers that her mother has been actively turning others against her that Tara accepts the trip was a mistake.

When Tara's parents ostracize her, they claim that she is a corrupting and dangerous force in the family. This claim reflects the fact that she has become a threat to the reality that Gene and Faye want to represent. While Tara persists in raising the issue of Shawn's bullying, she is failing to keep the unwritten family contract which demands that she ignore her brother's troubling behavioural problems. In shunning Tara, Gene and Faye also ensure that they get the support of Audrey, Luke and Shawn – all of whom are financially dependent upon them. Audrey's concurrence with her parents' point of view is one of the cruellest blows for Tara, as it was she who originally began the process of confronting Shawn's abusive behaviour. Her change of heart is a clear illustration of the pressure her parents have exerted on her.

When Tara becomes estranged from her parents and some of her siblings, the grief she feels is close to a bereavement. She does, however, maintain a close relationship with Tyler, Richard, and Tony – all of whom are mentioned in the acknowledgements of *Educated*. She also gets to know her maternal aunts and uncles – the siblings her mother distanced herself from years earlier when she married Gene. From the wreckage of her shattered family, we see Tara claiming a new one. She also has the consolation of those friends she has met in the course of her education. Acting as a surrogate family, Tara's friends provide the acceptance and support that she rarely received from her own parents.

By the end of her memoir, Westover concludes that, although the rift with her family remains a source of sadness, it has also brought her "peace." While she still misses her parents, she feels relieved that her life is no longer dominated by this dysfunctional relationship.

History

Tara first becomes aware of her lack of historical knowledge when she tries to read Tyler's copy of Les Misérables and cannot work out which parts are fiction and which historical fact. In Tara's eyes, Napoleon is just as likely to be a fictional character as Jean Valjean, for she has never heard of either of them.

The large gaps in Tara's understanding of the past are further demonstrated when she goes to college. In an art history lesson, she puts her hand up and asks the meaning of the word "Holocaust". Shocked at learning the facts about this mass genocide of the Jewish people, Tara cannot believe that, up until this moment, she has been completely oblivious to its occurrence.

Faced with how little she knows, Tara realizes that an individual's understanding of history depends on the information they have access to. In her case, she has grown up with her father's version of history which omits a great deal and is skewed to his own view of the world. His reasons for failing to mention the Holocaust, for example, become a little clearer when he later declares (in the middle of a crowded restaurant) that World War II and the Holocaust were engineered by Jewish bankers. By this stage, Tara knows enough to recognize these views from *The Protocols of the Elders of Zion*: a document which has long been discredited but was used to fuel anti-Semitism prior to World War II. Hearing her father voice this astonishing claim, Tara finds it incredible that she used to unquestioningly believe everything he said.

Tara also grows up largely unaware of the USA's fraught racial history. Although she often hears her family use the word "Nigger" as an insult, she never dwells on its meaning. Meanwhile, in her father's favoured history book, she reads that slaves were happier than their masters. It is only when Tara goes to BYU that she learns the horrific facts about the slave trade and that the problems of black Americans did not end with the abolition of slavery. In this new context, Tara reappraises her family's casually racist language: "a thousand times I had been called Nigger, and laughed, and now I could not laugh."

Another lesson that Tara learns about history is that information passed down as 'fact' is not necessarily correct. All stories about the past are prone to error as they involve the subjective perception of the teller. This point is neatly illustrated in the different versions of the Ruby Ridge siege. As a child, Tara is so deeply affected by her father's account of the siege that she begins to relive it in her head. Developing a false memory, she sees her own family in the place of the Weavers and imagines herself holding a baby. Years later, Tara is to learn that her false memory was based on another inaccurate account, as her father's retelling of the siege was also flawed. Influenced by his own paranoid view of the world, Gene misremembers the facts to reflect his own mistrust of the government.

Increasingly aware of the way her life has been shaped by inaccurate stories, Tara becomes interested in how historians negotiate issues such as subjectivity when interpreting the past. As a result, she specializes in historiography – the study of how historians come to their conclusions.

Meanwhile, in Buck's Peak, Tara's parents continue to demonstrate a talent for reinventing history. Following the incident where Shawn kills his dog and presents Tara with the bloodied knife, Gene and Faye construct an entirely different version of events, claiming that Tara's memory is unreliable. Initially, Faye suggests that Shawn gave his sister the knife to make her "feel more comfortable". She then progresses to denying that Shawn ever had a knife at all. Knowing that her parents will tell their version of the story to her siblings, Tara resigns herself to losing them all. In the face of her parents' "overpowering" narrative, she also begins to doubt whether she is able to trust her own memories and perception of events.

By drawing attention to the subjectivity of most historical accounts, Westover acknowledges that her own memoir also falls into this category. In writing it, however, she asserts her right to tell her own version of the facts without being overwhelmed by the counter-histories of her parents.

Religion

Tara Westover was brought up in a Mormon household and her memoir illustrates the impact of her father's faith on his family. In her "Author's Note", however, she asserts that *Educated* is not about Mormonism or any other religion. Emphasizing that her father was "a religious extremist", she tells readers not to look to her story for a portrait of a typical Mormon family. While the Westovers lived in a Mormon community, their lifestyle was not representative of the whole.

Gene's take on Mormonism is heavily influenced by his extreme (possibly bipolar) personality traits. The issue is not religious doctrine itself but the way that he interprets it to suit his own view of the world. Many Mormons believe in the Second Coming, but Gene makes practical preparations for it with undisguised glee. Mormons are also encouraged to develop a personal relationship with God in order to guide and direct their families. In Gene's case, however, he believes this process makes his own word synonymous with that of God. When, for example, Tara announces that she wants to go to school, Gene's own displeasure is reflected in his claim that she is provoking the wrath of God. Similarly, when Gene claims that Shawn has been cleansed of sin and tries to force Tara and Audrey into forgiving their brother, he proclaims they will be defying "God's will" if they refuse.

Westover conveys how her father's religious zeal is a source of some amusement within the Mormon community, describing how he is gently teased about his preparations for the end of the world. As a child, Tara is also shown to take some of Gene's more bizarre proclamations with a pinch of salt – sneaking over to her grandmother's house for milk when her father suddenly decides that it is the work of the devil. A less amusing aspect of her father's preaching is his draconian attitude towards women. Gene's extreme views about feminine modesty are illustrated when he attends Tara's dance recital and describes the dancers (who are all Mormons) as "jumping about like whores". Gene's shocking perception of the young girls as sinfully sexualized is reflected in Tara's initial assessment of her classmates as "tiny harlots". Growing up hearing her father's rants about women who tempt men by wearing provocative clothing, Tara internalizes his misogynist ideas on how a woman should look and behave. This leads to feelings of self-loathing when she reaches adolescence.

While her father's views are at the extreme end of the scale, Tara gradually comes to question the prescribed gender roles perpetuated by the Mormon faith. As a child, she is taught that the number of wives a man has in the afterlife increases in direct proportion to his "righteousness". Pious Mormon women, however, receive the dubious reward of becoming one of many "sister wives" in the hereafter. Although polygamy is no longer widely practiced among the Mormon community, Tara also struggles with the fact that the Church has never officially retracted its stance on multiple marriages. Her doubts come to a head when she experiences a crisis over the subjects she should study. While her religion initially draws her to the 'feminine' study of music, her intellect increasingly pulls her towards more traditionally 'masculine' areas of thought. The gender stereotyping she struggles with is further illustrated when a male Mormon friend declares that there would be something wrong with a woman if she wanted to study law.

While Tara does not officially break with her religion in *Educated*, she illustrates the conflict between what the Mormon church teaches her she should be and who she actually is. It is no great surprise to learn that Westover no longer considers herself a Mormon, declaring "I tried to be a Mormon feminist but that was exhausting."

Power & Abuse

In the Westover household, Gene and Shawn wield power over the rest of the family. Between them, Tara's father and brother create a particularly toxic form of patriarchal rule, dominating family life and continuing to exert influence on Tara, even when she leaves for college.

As the head of his Mormon household, Gene feels he has the authority to dictate to his family on all aspects of life. Ruling with a rod of iron, he uses his patriarchal role to ensure that his wife and children go along with his every whim. On the rare occasions when his authority is challenged, he often resorts to exploiting his children's financial dependence upon him. When, for example, he is unable to talk Tara out of her plan to go to college, he begins charging her for random utilities and threatens to throw her out of the house. If all else fails, he falls back on temper tantrums – as is demonstrated in the scene where Faye and Tara return home after securing her university accommodation. Furious that his will has been thwarted, Gene launches into an angry rant, accusing Tara of disconnecting the VCR cables. Automatically, Tara responds to her father's unreasonable rage by trying to appease him, anxiously trying to reconnect the cables as he continues to shout. When, in a moment of clarity, she drops the cables and walks out of the room, Faye takes her daughter's place. The image of Tara's mother "groping for the wires, as Dad towered over her" perfectly summarizes the dynamics in the Westover household.

Gene's dictatorial manner becomes even more tyrannical in the environment of the junkyard. Every one of the Westover children must go through the rite of working in Gene's domain and he proves a harsh and unreasonable taskmaster. The full extent of Gene's megalomania is shockingly illustrated after Shawn refuses to work the lethal-looking Shear. Humiliated by his elder son's insubordination, Gene then forces Luke and Tara to use the machine to reassert his authority. As Luke is injured within minutes, Gene makes Tara take his place with the machine still covered in her brother's blood. This distressing scene seems to suggest that Gene would rather sacrifice his children than lose his authority over them.

As the incident with the Shear highlights, Shawn is the only one of Gene's children to consistently (and often successfully) challenge his father's authority. Unfortunately, he also exerts an insidious and tyrannical power of his own.

While Shawn engages in a power struggle with Gene, he finds an easier target in young women. It is his girlfriends and his sisters (once they reach adolescence) who receive the full force of his abuse. Physically violent, he uses his size and strength to overpower the women in his life. Perhaps more damaging still, however, is the emotional damage he inflicts through vindictive cruelties, verbal abuse and humiliation.

Westover brings home the impact of Shawn's abuse by illustrating how he succeeds in defining Tara to herself. His repeated claim that she is a "whore" mars her future relationships with men. Meanwhile, no matter how impressive her academic achievements, she associates herself with the girl who had her head shoved down the toilet and her underwear exposed in a parking lot.

One of the most disturbing aspects of Shawn's abusive behaviour is the way that his parents facilitate it. Unable to control him, Faye and Gene turn a blind eye when he terrorizes his sisters and they actively discourage their children from raising the issue. Their determination to avoid the truth grants Shawn further power, placing him in the position where he can have his siblings ousted from the family. This is precisely what happens to Tara when she dares to speak the truth about Shawn's actions.

As a child, Tara feels the effects of the power dynamics of her family without being able to analyse them. One of the advantages of her education is that it gives her the vocabulary to define what is happening. Before reading feminist theory at Cambridge, Tara has only ever heard the term "feminist" as an insult in her home. As she becomes familiar with feminist thought on the role of patriarchy in oppressing women, she realizes that this is exactly what takes place in her own home. Learning about the history of black oppression also makes her aware of the role language can play in the dynamics of power. Now understanding the demeaning and dehumanizing connotations of the word "Nigger", she recognizes Shawn's motivation in calling her this. Ultimately, Tara's education gives her the tools to identify and challenge these abuses of power.

Accidents & Healing

There are many extraordinary aspects of Tara's childhood narrative. Perhaps the most astonishing of all is the number of serious accidents that she and her family are involved in. In the course of her memoir, the Westovers experience two serious car crashes, three life-threatening industrial accidents and a number of other wince-inducing scrapyard related injuries. Although the frequency of these accidents is quite breath-taking there is no real mystery over why they happen. While Gene devotes a great deal of energy into protecting his family from the corruption of the world, he displays an astonishingly cavalier attitude to keeping them physically safe.

Gene's approach to workplace safety is illustrated when ten-year-old Tara reports for her first day as "crew" in the scrapyard. Gene immediately removes his daughter's gloves and hard hat, claiming that they will slow her down. Assuring Tara that "God and his angels" will protect her, he proceeds to throw sheets of metal across the yard, apparently forgetting that she is in their path.

Work in the scrapyard becomes even more hazardous when Gene brings home a terrifying-looking machine called 'the Shear'. With huge motorized jaws, the Shear is so powerful that it can easily pull whoever is using it into the blades. While Shawn labels the cutting contraption a "death machine", Gene is like a child with a new toy and revels in its lethal capacity. Within five minutes of using it, Luke is incapacitated by a gash to his arm. Gene then orders Tara to step up. Seeing her brother's blood on the Shear, Tara prays for an injury no worse than Luke's so that she can go back to the house and be tended to by her mother. In the end, however, it is Shawn who saves her by taking over when he sees his sister thrown to the floor by the force of the Shear. Gene's determination to make every one of his children work the Shear comes to represent his complete disregard for their safety. Later in life, Tara realizes that her lack of self-worth largely arises "from having a father who shoved me toward the chomping blades of the shear, instead of pulling me away from them."

Relatively speaking, Tara is fortunate as the most serious injury she sustains is a deeply gashed leg and damaged kidney after her father orders her to climb onto a huge forklift. Her brother, Luke, is not so lucky. While working for his father, Luke accidentally sets himself alight and suffers horrific burns to his leg. His injuries are made worse by the fact that, instead of protective clothing, he is wearing jeans held up with baling twine and duct-taped boots. Neither can be easily removed and his jeans melt, leaving his skin "like wax dripping from a cheap candle."

Even Shawn – not known for his cautious nature - complains about his father's dangerous working methods. He then becomes a victim of them when he falls twenty feet from a raised wooden pallet and lands headfirst on a concrete wall. Despite the severity of his fall, Gene leaves his son to 'rest', while he and his crew continue with the job. It is only when Shawn starts screaming and attacks Gene that they summon the emergency services. By this time, Shawn has suffered another blow to the head, sustained as Gene and his crew subdued him. As calling an ambulance is an unprecedented event in the Westover household, Tara can only imagine how "chilling" Shawn's condition must have been. Doctors surmise that Shawn was already in a critical condition when he was concussed for a second time. Astonishingly, however, he survives and goes on to receive several more head injuries at the hands of the Shear.

Tara's father has a similarly lax attitude towards the safety of his family when it comes to driving. Seatbelts are redundant, and Gene seems to get a kick out of taking a Russian Roulette approach to family car journeys. After he decides, on the spur of the moment, that they will drive home from Arizona through the night, Tyler falls asleep at the wheel, colliding with a tractor and electricity pylons. Everyone is injured in the crash and Faye fares worst of all, suffering terrible facial contusions. Clearly suffering from a brain injury, she is never quite the same again, experiencing headaches and memory loss. As a result, Tyler feels a huge burden of guilt over the accident. Gene, however, shows no sign that he feels responsible for his wife's suffering.

Gene demonstrates that he has learned nothing when, during a second trip to Arizona, he again announces that they will drive home through the night – this time through a snowstorm. When Richard pulls over, declaring the conditions too bad to continue, Gene takes the wheel and drives like a maniac. In this moment, Westover powerfully conveys the fear and helplessness of being in the hands of a father who continually courts danger. With no doubt in her mind that they are going to crash, she declares "It is a relief when the van finally leaves the road." In the aftermath of the accident, no one takes Gene to task for his recklessness. Instead, Westover recalls, "We didn't look at Dad, didn't want to accuse." The enormity of this statement illustrates just how frightened Gene's family are of arousing his displeasure.

Gene's disregard for danger is compounded by his aversion to pharmaceuticals and the medical establishment. Readers are left wondering how any of the Westover clan survived as Gene insists that his family are treated only with Faye's herbal remedies (created through the strange, finger-clicking process of "muscle testing"). Faced with an injured child, it would be the instinct of most parents to seek professional medical help. Gene's reaction, however, is quite the reverse. After Luke's accident, he instructs his children not to tell anyone about it, claiming that Luke will die of an infection if he is taken to the hospital.

To those of us who trust in conventional medicine, Gene's faith in homeopathy seems naïve and even irresponsible. It cannot be denied, however, that, despite the serious injuries they suffer, the Westovers seem to respond extremely well to Faye's herbal remedies. Whether this is a testament to the body's incredible capacity for self-healing or to Faye's talents as a herbalist, it is difficult to say. In Gene's favour, he does at least demonstrate the courage of his convictions after accidentally setting fire to himself at work. Although the accident badly burns his hands and leaves the "lower half of his face liquefied", Gene refuses Faye's offer to take him to the hospital. Instead, he submits to having his dead skin scraped away with a butter knife and puts faith in the salve his wife smothers him in. Considering the severity of his injuries, Gene's recovery under Faye's care is remarkable. Six months after the accident, Tara has to wonder if trained medical professionals could have achieved the same results.

Once it is clear that Gene will survive, it is generally agreed that his recovery is miraculous, and Faye's recipe becomes known as

'Miracle Salve.' From then on, Tara's parents begin to present Gene's accident and his recovery as a badge of honour. Gene interprets it as a sign that he has been chosen by God to demonstrate that faith is more powerful than any conventional medicine. Faye, meanwhile, becomes convinced that God is working through her hands, going on to claim that she can prevent heart attacks and cure cancer.

By insisting on a connection between his religious faith and his miraculous recovery, Gene finds a convenient way to make sense of the injuries suffered by his family. Instead of facing the fact that the car crashes and succession of workplace accidents are his fault, he interprets them as part of God's great plan. In this scheme of things, every near miss becomes further proof of his piousness. When Emily almost dies giving birth to her daughter, for example, Gene and Faye proclaim the incident to be "a testament of His power." Meanwhile, Tara recalls Emily's first premature labour and reflects that to encourage her to have her second child at home "seemed reckless to the point of delusion."

The snowballing success of Faye's herbal remedy business leads to Tara's parents becoming one of the wealthiest and biggest employers in the county. This is an ironic development as Tara reveals her mother did not always share her husband's absolute faith in herbal remedies - once stating (out of Gene's hearing) that, "Herbs are supplements. For something serious, you should go to a doctor."

Significantly, Tara's attitude toward medicine changes as her memoir progresses. As a child, she does not question the idea that prescription drugs are "an abomination to God". After hitting her head in a car accident, she is more afraid of being taken to the hospital than a brain injury. For this reason, she does not admit to the ambulance crew that she lost consciousness, enduring weeks of paralysing headaches instead. Only when Tara is a college student does she reluctantly accept a painkiller from Charles when her mother's tincture of lobelia and skullcap has no effect on her excruciating earache. Later, another boyfriend, Nick, persuades her to visit a clinic for the first time where she accepts penicillin for a throat infection. Finally, she goes ahead and has her vaccinations.

Tara's slow acceptance of the medical establishment reflects her gradual shedding of her parents' influence on her. The real turning point, however, comes when she is forced to make a spur-of-the-moment decision about Shawn. When Shawn hits a cow on his motorcycle, he suffers a head injury so deep it reveals his brain. Calling her father and explaining the extent of Shawn's injuries, Tara receives the predictable response that she should bring him home. At this moment, however, Tara remembers her father's reaction to Shawn's previous serious head injury and questions his judgement. Ignoring Gene's instructions, she drives Shawn to the hospital. Afterwards, Gene does not comment on Tara's disobedience but refuses to look at her. It is then that Tara realizes there is no going back from this rebellion. From this point, she commits herself to leaving Buck's Peak.

SYMBOLISM

Buck's Peak

When describing the mountain that looms on the horizon of her childhood home, Westover often uses personification. The mountain's changing landscape through the seasons is likened to the changing expressions of a face and, in windy weather, it is "as if the peak itself is exhaling." This reflects Tara's perception of Buck's Peak as a living presence.

Tara and her family revere the mountain like a deity and, significantly, Buck's Peak is always referred to as "she". Gene calls part of the mountain "the Indian Princess", as its rocky outline resembles a woman's face. Tara, meanwhile, sees an entire female figure in the landscape: "her legs formed of huge ravines, her hair a spray of pines fanning over the northern ridge." This commanding female presence on the horizon is a reminder of the innate power of women, providing a refreshing contrast to life within the Westover household where patriarchy rules.

Throughout Westover's memoir, the mountain remains a symbol of home. Even when thousands of miles away, Tara feels the absence of the Indian Princess on the skyline.

The Railway Car

As a child, Tara is drawn to the old abandoned railway car that stands in her father's scrapyard. Sitting on top of it, she imagines speeding into the distance. As this railway car has come to the end of its travelling days, Tara's childhood game emphasizes the fact that she is stuck in Buck's Peak without much hope of escaping. The wrecked vehicle takes on new symbolism, however, when Tara fulfils her fantasy, travelling across the U.S. and to Europe in her educational quest.

Wild Animals

During Tara's childhood, her family try to break feral horses from the mountains. Despite all attempts to tame them, however, the horses remain wild. When Tara finally gets to ride her first domestic horse, she is surprised at how quickly he tolerates a saddle. Having never known a life in the wild, Bud automatically accepts the limited parameters of his world.

In a similar incident, Tara describes her family's attempts to rescue an injured great horned owl. Although Faye tries to treat the bird, it grows restless, refusing food, and they are forced to release the owl before it is fully recovered.

In both anecdotes, the wild creatures are unable to accept the restraints of domesticity: the call of the wild is too great for them to resist. This wild instinct mirrors the way Tara comes to feel about her life at Buck's Peak as she feels the call of a larger, more expansive horizon. While it would be easier to accept the restrictions of her life, as Bud does, Tara ultimately cannot be "owned".

Judith Beheading Holofernes

When Tara takes a Western Civilization class at BYU, she is shown a series of works of art during a test. Unable to identify any of the paintings accurately, her greatest insight is that Judith's serene expression in Caravaggio's *Judith Beheading Holofernes* is unrealistic. Basing this on her own experience of beheading chickens, she knows that serenity is an impossible state to attain when blood and feathers are flying everywhere. This humorous anecdote illustrates the gaping holes in Tara's cultural knowledge and also the chasm between her experiences and those of her fellow students.

Several years later, Tara sees Caravaggio's masterpiece in a gallery in Rome. The fact that she can look at the painting and "not once think about chickens" reflects just how far she has travelled in her educational journey.

The Legend of the Apache Tears

When Tara is a child, her paternal grandmother tells her the legend of the Apache tears. This piece of local folk lore recounts a battle that took place a hundred years earlier between a tribe of Apaches and the U.S. Cavalry. The story goes that, hopelessly outnumbered and trapped, the Apache warriors chose to ride off the edge of the mountain to their deaths rather than suffer the dishonour of being captured. Afterwards, when the Apache women found the bodies of their men, their tears turned to stone. The legend does not specify what happened to the Apache women after this point and Tara reflects "A slaughter was the likely outcome of the warriors' bravery. They died as heroes, their wives as slaves."

The author strongly identifies with the legend of the Apache tears as she is also raised in an environment where a woman's fate is determined by men. The image of the Apache men dashing to their deaths, leaving their women to suffer the consequences, brings to mind Gene's suicidal decisions to drive home through the night from Arizona. At the mercy of his reckless whims, his family narrowly escape death and his wife suffers a brain injury.

Clothing

Throughout the memoir, Tara is shown to have ambiguous feelings about her personal appearance. Indoctrinated with Gene and Shawn's draconian ideas on how a 'modest' woman should look, it is little wonder that she feels conflicted about the way she presents herself.

Gene's extreme views on appropriate female attire are illustrated in a scene where Tara is working in the scrapyard on a hot day. Following the lead of Luke, who rips his shirt to cool himself down, Tara rolls up the sleeves of her T-shirt exposing a small portion of her shoulders. While Luke's actions go unremarked upon, Gene immediately pulls his daughter's sleeves down, proclaiming "This ain't a whorehouse". Although Gene expects Tara to work like a man she must, on no account, bare the same amount of flesh.

On this occasion, Tara defies her father by rolling her sleeves back up again. There are many other instances, however, when she is shown to have internalized her father's views about what a woman should wear. On first seeing her ballet classmates dancing in their leotards and tights, Tara assesses them as "tiny harlots". Years later, she is outraged when she sees the word "Juicy" emblazoned on her BYU housemate's pyjama bottoms.

Tara's anxieties over her appearance come to a head when she begins dating Charles. Suddenly aware of how unflattering her shapeless men's clothes are, she buys women's jeans. Afterwards, she agonizes over wearing them, feeling it is wrong to draw attention to the shape of her body.

At Trinity College, Cambridge, clothes become an issue for Tara once again. Her belief that she does not belong in this hallowed environment is compounded by the feeling that she is always inappropriately clad. During a black-tie dinner (for which she wears a black shirt and pants) she shows that she remains her father's daughter when she judges a friend's above-the-knee dress to be "whorish". She is then forced to reconsider her assessment when she learns that the dress, bought in Paris, was a gift from her friend's father. Struggling to correlate the two things in her mind she reasons that "A gift from one's father could not be whorish."

Suffering from impostor syndrome at Cambridge, Tara cannot envision herself wearing a Cambridge graduate's robes. Dr. Kerry, meanwhile, tries to convince her to believe in her own merit, reminding her that Pygmalion "was just a Cockney in a nice dress. Until she believed in herself. Then it didn't matter what dress she wore."

Looking at publicity shots of Tara Westover now, it is hard to believe that the elegant woman in these photographs once wore shapeless men's clothes and turned up to her first ballet class in steel-toed boots. Favouring beautifully cut clothes and bright lipstick, the author finally appears confident in the image she projects to the world. She is, however, quick to point out that "The way I dress now is the least powerful thing about how much I have changed. You could put me back in those same clothes I wore when I was 16 but I wouldn't think the way I did then."

DISCUSSION QUESTIONS

1/ Tara Westover grows up in the isolated rural area of Buck's Peak in Idaho. What impact does this environment have on her? How does she feel about the Indian Princess? The scrapyard?

2/ Tara's father, Gene, is a survivalist, religious extremist, and harbours paranoid delusions about the American government. What impact does this eclectic mixture of beliefs have on Tara as she grows up?

3/ Discuss the episode, in Part One, Chapter 5, where grandma-over-in-town introduces Tara to the concept of washing her hands after using the bathroom. What does it illustrate about Tara at this point? Discuss how Tara's perception of her maternal grandmother changes later in her memoir.

4/ In her 'Author's Note' Westover claims that her memoir is not about Mormonism or "any form of religious belief". What does she mean by this? Which aspects of Mormon teaching does Tara struggle with? How is this reflected in her feelings about her great-great-grandmother, Anna Mathea?

5/ As a small child, Tara absorbs her father's opinions like a sponge. As she grows older, however, she forms new ideas and begins to shed the ingrained beliefs of her father. Discuss some of the turning points in Tara's battle for self-assertion and independence of thought.

6/ Faye is a submissive wife. She also goes on to become a hugely successful businesswoman and the major breadwinner of the Westover family. Discuss these two opposing sides to her character. Do you think she truly shares her husband's opinions and beliefs? If not, why does she fail to stand up to Gene?

7/ Tara's brothers, Tyler and Shawn, both have influence over her but in completely different ways. How does Tyler help to transform Tara's sense of who she might become? Discuss the way that Shawn's arrival undermines much of Tyler's good work.

8/ In the course of Westover's memoir, her family suffers an astonishing number of accidents and near misses (two serious car accidents, numerous workplace injuries and two dangerous home births). Discuss the cause of these incidents. How does Gene explain them, and how does his attitude relate to the legend of the Apache tears?

9/ Gene's abhorrence of doctors and pharmaceuticals means that all the Westovers' ailments are treated with Faye's herbal remedies. Did it surprise you that they all survived? Is this a testament to Faye's powers as a healer or could there be some other explanation (e.g. the body's natural healing process or the placebo effect)? How does Faye's attitude to medicine and healing change as the memoir goes on? How does Tara's?

10/ When Tara arrives at BYU she becomes aware of how little her parents have prepared her for the outside world. Discuss the steep learning curve she has to go through – inside and outside of the classroom. Also, what practical issues does she have to overcome to stay at BYU?

11/ As Tara has a troubled relationship with her parents and Shawn, going to college provides the perfect opportunity to distance herself from them. Nevertheless, she persists in returning to Buck's Peak again and again. What is it that draws her back?

12/ At college, Tara goes through a process of rapid change but reverts to her old self when she returns to her childhood home. She also notices this phenomenon in her brother Richard, who waver's between being his "wife's husband" and "his father' son". Do you think most of us revert to our childhood selves to some degree in the presence of our parents?

13/ One of the lessons that Tara learns at BYU is that a person's understanding of history depends upon the information they have access to. Discuss some examples of how Tara's upbringing has limited her understanding of history and the world in general.

14/ When Tara reads newspaper accounts of the Ruby Ridge siege she discovers that they differ from the version that Gene told her as a child. Why is she so angry when she discovers the discrepancies in her father's story? Do you think Gene's distortion of the truth was deliberate?

15/ After learning about the symptoms of bipolar disorder (paranoia, depression, delusions of grandeur etc.), Tara begins to suspect that her father may suffer from this mental illness. Do you think, from the evidence the author presents, that she is right? If so, can Gene really be held responsible for his behaviour and its impact?

16/ On a tour of a chapel roof at the University of Cambridge, Dr. Kerry observes how Tara stands straight and confident while the other students cower in the wind. How does Tara interpret Dr. Kerry's observation? What does the incident really illustrate about Tara's character?

17/ At Cambridge, Tara receives indisputable confirmation that she is a talented scholar. Why does she find this so difficult to accept?

18/ In Harper Lee's *To Kill a Mockingbird*, Jem famously declares, "You can choose your friends but you sho' can't choose your family". With this in mind, discuss the way that Tara accumulates an alternative family in *Educated*. What role do people like Charles, Robin, the bishop, Dr. Kerry, and Professor Steinberg play in her life?

19/ Westover's memoir revolves around the conflict between her desire to be educated and her loyalties towards her family. What is it that makes Tara's education incompatible with maintaining a relationship with her parents? Why does Tara find it so hard to accept that this is the case?

20/ While Tara's relationship with her parents deteriorates

gradually, the moment of no return comes when she confronts them about Shawn's abusive behaviour. Discuss the way that, up until this point, Tara and her parents have colluded with Shawn's abuse. Why does Tara decide that she can no longer do so? Why do you think Gene and Faye are so determined to cover up for Shawn?

21/ In her memoir, Westover strives to answer two questions: what is an education, and what is its value? How does Tara's attitude towards education change as the narrative progresses? What does she ultimately conclude about the value of an education?

22/ In marrying Gene, Faye rebelled against the respectability of her parents. Meanwhile, despite Gene's disapproval of formal education, three of his children go on to study for doctorates. From your own experience, do you think that most of us kick against the values of our parents, or crave what we miss out on in childhood? Is this an important part of what shapes us?

23/ Writing *Educated* was a therapeutic process for the author but has made reconciliation with her parents even less likely. Although she has given her estranged family members pseudonyms, it is relatively easy to find out their identities and the book has received a hostile reception in these quarters. Do you think Tara Westover did the right thing in exposing her family history? Would you have done the same in her position?

24/ In many ways, *Educated* reads more like a novel than a memoir. Discuss the stylistic features that make it stand out from more run-of-the-mill autobiographies.

25/ By drawing attention to the biased nature of most accounts of the past, Westover acknowledges that her own story is also told from a subjective point of view. Were there any parts of the memoir where you questioned her version of events? Why, or why not? Does it matter if her account is one hundred percent accurate? If you were writing your own life story, how objective do you think you would be?

26/ *Educated* joins the ranks of a number of bestselling memoirs that describe growing up within poor American communities (*Hillbilly Elegy*, *The Glass Castle*, etc.) Why do you think there has been a recent boom in this kind of memoir? What do we gain from reading them? Would these stories be just as gripping if they were not based on true events?

QUIZ QUESTIONS

1/ How many siblings does Tara have, and what are their names?

2/ After a 'revelation from God', What type of food product does Gene ban from his home?

3/ Why does Faye have difficulty getting a Delayed Certificate of Birth for Tara?

4/ When Luke accidentally sets himself on fire, how does Tara cool down his horrifically burned leg?

5/ When Tara first goes to dance classes she sums up her impression of her classmates in two words. What are they?

6/ Which musical does Tara land the starring role in?

7/ What nickname does Shawn give to his girlfriend, Sadie (implying she is beautiful but vacant)?

8/ When Tara repeatedly suffers from swollen tonsils, what is her father's medical advice?

9/ Which comic literary character does the author compare her father to?

10/ What does Gene predict will happen on 31 December 1999 at midnight?

11/ When a car accident leaves Faye with dark rings around her eyes, what do her children call her? What does Tara later find out about this 'humorous' nickname?

12/ Tara is shocked when she discovers that her father's account of the Ruby Ridge siege does not match with the recorded facts. Which parts of Gene's version prove to be inaccurate?

13/ Which illness does Tara begin to suspect her father suffers from?

14/ Towards the end of the memoir, Shawn confronts Tara with a bloodied knife. Who does the blood belong to?

15/ Which of her siblings is Tara still in contact with by the end of her memoir?

QUIZ ANSWERS

1/ Six: Tyler, Shawn, Tony, Luke, Audrey and Richard

2/ Milk

3/ Because no one in the family can agree on which day she was born

4/ She stands him in a garbage bin full of water

5/ "tiny harlots"

6/ *Annie*

7/ Fish Eyes

8/ To stand with her mouth open in the sunshine for at least half an hour each day

9/ Don Quixote

10/ He expects electricity to fail, the world to fall into chaos and the Days of Abomination to begin

11/ "Racoon Eyes". Tara later discovers this is a medical term to describe a symptom of brain damage.

12/ He claims that all the Weaver family were killed when, in fact, Randy Weaver and three of his daughters survived. He also claims that the family were targeted for homeschooling their children when, the truth is, they were under surveillance due to Randy's criminal activities and links to a white supremacist movement.

13/ Bipolar disorder

14/ Diego – Shawn's German Shepherd

15/ Tyler, Richard and Tony

FURTHER READING

The Glass Castle by Jeannette Walls

Hillbilly Elegy by J.D. Vance

The Liar's Club by Mary Karr

In the Days of Rain by Rebecca Stott

I Know Why the Caged Bird Sings by Maya Angelou

Stolen Innocence by Elissa Wall

Why Be Happy When You Could Be Normal? by Jeanette Winterson

The Great Alone by Kristin Hannah

History of Wolves by Emily Fridlund

My Name is Lucy Barton by Elizabeth Strout

FURTHER TITLES IN THIS SERIES

Alias Grace (Margaret Atwood): A Guide for Book Clubs

Beartown (Fredrik Backman): A Guide for Book Clubs

Before We Were Yours (Lisa Wingate) A Guide for Book Clubs

Big Little Lies (Liane Moriarty): A Guide for Book Clubs

The Book Thief (Markus Zusak): A Guide for Book Clubs

Commonwealth (Ann Patchett): A Guide for Book Clubs

The Fault in Our Stars (John Green): A Guide for Book Clubs

Frankenstein (Mary Shelley): A Guide for Book Clubs

A Gentleman in Moscow (Amor Towles): A Guide for Book Clubs

The Girl on the Train (Paula Hawkins): A Guide for Book Clubs

Go Set a Watchman (Harper Lee): A Guide for Readers

A God in Ruins (Kate Atkinson): A Guide for Book Clubs

The Goldfinch (Donna Tartt): A Guide for Book Clubs

Gone Girl (Gillian Flynn): A Guide for Book Clubs

The Great Alone (Kristin Hannah) A Guide for Book Clubs

The Great Gatsby (F. Scott Fitzgerald): A Guide for Book Clubs

The Grownup (Gillian Flynn): A Guide for Book Clubs

The Guernsey Literary and Potato Peel Pie Society (Mary Ann Shaffer & Annie Burrows): A Guide for Book Clubs

The Heart Goes Last (Margaret Atwood): A Guide for Book Clubs

The Husband's Secret (Liane Moriarty): A Guide for Book Clubs

I Know Why the Caged Bird Sings (Maya Angelou): A Guide for Book Clubs

The Light between Oceans (M.L. Stedman): A Guide for Book Clubs

Lincoln in the Bardo (George Saunders): A Guide for Book Clubs

Little Fires Everywhere (Celeste Ng): A Guide for Book Clubs

My Brilliant Friend (Elena Ferrante): A Guide for Book Clubs

My Name is Lucy Barton (Elizabeth Strout): A Guide for Book Clubs

The Narrow Road to the Deep North (Richard Flanagan): A Guide for Book Clubs

The Paying Guests (Sarah Waters): A Guide for Book Clubs

The Secret History (Donna Tartt): A Guide for Book Clubs

The Storied Life of A.J. Fikry (Gabrielle Zevin): A Guide for Book Clubs

The Sympathizer (Viet Thanh Nguyen): A Guide for Book Clubs

The Underground Railroad (Colson Whitehead): A Guide for Book Clubs

BIBLIOGRAPHY

Tara Westover. *Educated: A Memoir*. Random House, 2018

Carey, Anna. (February 2018). "Educated by Tara Westover review: An extraordinary Mormon upbringing recounted with evocative lyricism." *The Irish Times*.

Carpenter, Louise (February 2018). "Tara Westover: the Mormon who didn't go to school (but now has a Cambridge PhD)." *The Times*.

Conroy, Catherine. (February 2018). "You could miss someone every day and still be glad they're not in your life." *The Irish Times*.

Dean, Michelle. (February 2018). "Educated by Tara Westover review – escape from a Mormon fundamentalist family." *The Guardian*.

Harrison, Melissa. (February 2018). "Educated by Tara Westover — more than just survival". *Financial Times*.

Hertzel, Laurie. (February 2018). "Review: 'Educated,' by Tara Westover". *Star Tribune*.

Hurlburt, Ann (March 2018). "Educated Is a Brutal, One-of-a-Kind Memoir (book review)". *The Atlantic*.

Layman, Alex (February 2018). "Tara Westover." *KIRKUS*.

O'Kelly, Lisa. (February 2018). "Tara Westover: 'In families like mine there is no crime worse than telling the truth". *The Guardian*.

Sanderson, Caroline. (February 2018). "Tara Westover: My biggest fear wasn't that it wouldn't get published but that it would get published when it didn't deserve to be." *The Bookseller*.

ABOUT THE AUTHOR

Kathryn Cope graduated in English Literature from Manchester University and obtained her master's degree in contemporary fiction from the University of York. She is the author of Study Guides for Book Clubs and the HarperCollins Official Book Club series. She lives in the Staffordshire Moorlands with her husband, son and dog.

www.amazon.com/author/kathryncope